KATE VENTER

Sugar Decorating

FILIGREE, FLOWERS & FLOODING

MEREHURST PRESS

LONDON

Published 1987 by Merehurst Press
5 Great James Street
London WC1N 3DA
First edition 1987

© 1987 Tafelberg Publishers Ltd

ISBN 0 948075 75 9

Designed by G & G Design
Photography by Dick Bomford
Illustrations by Alice Howard
Set in 10 on 12 pt Plantin Monotype Lasercomp
Printed and bound by
Toppan Printing Company (H.K.) Ltd,
Hong Kong

Contents

Acknowledgements

Compiling a book of this nature requires long and thorough preparation, which one person is scarcely able to do.

I owe a great debt of gratitude, therefore, to a number of people who helped me: Cynthia Fletcher and Frances Bell, for their selfless help and assistance with embroidery and flooding; Irene Pienaar, Agata Pomario, Ina Goulden, Jackie Duncan, Gertie du Toit and Tineke Rosslee, who assisted with the making of blooms and other decorations; Henry Willis, who was always willing to make templates at short notice; and Margie Smuts, who designed all the filigree patterns and also assisted with the making of the decorations featured.

Thanks are due, too, to all those other people, among my students and friends, who helped in a variety of ways, to my sister and brothers, who supported me with advice, love and helping hands, and to the publishers, who made this second book in the series possible.

Above all, however, my thanks are offered to Him whose guidance in the execution of my work has been indispensable.

Recipes and special techniques

In *Sugar art*, to which this book is a sequel, the tried and tested recipes are given for fruit cakes and fondant, among others. But cake decorators generally have their own recipes or (in the case of fondant) use commercially available mixtures, so to repeat the recipes here would be superfluous. The technique of crimping, however, which is applied to cakes freshly covered with fondant, needs to be dealt with in detail.

Crimping

This technique, although relatively slow, is very effective for decorating the tops and sides of cakes. Special instruments called crimpers, which resemble large tweezers, are used (see *plate 1*).

Crimpers come in various shapes and sizes, and are used, for example, to make long, medium or short straight or curved lines, heart and diamond patterns, and so on.

Get patterns and templates ready before covering the cake with fondant, so that you can prick out and crimp the design immediately. If crimping is applied to fondant which has already become too hard, it will result in cracking or leave unsightly marks.

In addition, once a crimping imprint has been made, it cannot be removed. It would be best, therefore, to practise with whatever crimpers you intend using on a partly covered dummy cake before tackling the actual work.

Note: Do not practise on a flat surface, as the skill mastered in this way differs from that required for working at an angle.

Make sure that the crimper you are going to use is clean and completely dry. If it is not, the fondant will stick to it. To prevent this happening while you are working, dip the crimper in cornflour or fat at regular intervals.

Ensure that the prongs are about 5 mm apart and hold the crimper at right angles to the cake. Push the crimper into the fondant (not more than 3 mm deep), and squeeze until the prongs are approximately 1,5 mm apart. Release the pressure and allow the prongs to return to the 5 mm position. Remove the crimper.

Note: Remove the crimper when the gap between the prongs is exactly 5 mm wide – no more, no less. If it is removed at the wrong time, the crimper could pull out bits of the fondant or form holes.

A good idea would be to wind a rubber band or sticky tape around the crimper, about 20 mm from the front. Doing this would prevent its opening up more than 5 mm.

Crimping should always be overpiped, using either the main colour of the cake or one that complements it. Crimping combines well with inserted ribbons, dropped loops, and bridge, embroidery or lacework. *Plate 2* gives a few designs for you to use when decorating the sides and/or tops of cakes.

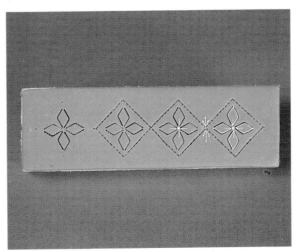

Plate 1
Crimpers (note how the prongs of those in front are kept the correct distance apart with adhesive tape)

Plate 2
Progressives of seven crimping designs (continued on page 10)

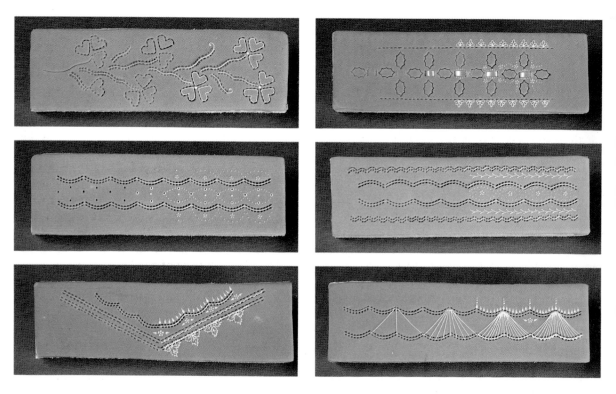

Filigree and lacework

Filigree and lacework are extremely intricate, delicate patterns piped with royal icing, using tubes Nos. 1, 0 or 00. An injection needle attached to a tube, can also be used. The piping is done on wax paper or a sheet of thin plastic (note: not cling film) secured over a pattern, and left to dry. It is then carefully removed and attached to the cake as a free-standing design.

Although some decorators finish off certain designs with cotton net or tulle, the result is far more striking and rewarding if filigree or lace made of royal icing is used.

Recipe for royal icing for filigree and bridge work

1 egg white, at room temperature
± 200 g (7 oz) icing sugar (± 400 ml)
5 ml (1 t) liquid glucose
2,5 ml (½ t) gum tragacanth or gum arabic

Strain the egg white through a dry muslin cloth to break it up without affecting its ability to thicken. Beat lightly.

Sift the icing sugar through a very fine sieve (a piece of organdie or nylon stocking could also be used). Add gradually to the egg white, stirring continuously. Add just enough icing sugar to obtain a mixture with a soft, creamy consistency. Mix in the glucose and gum.

Test: The mixture is the right consistency if a spoon dipped into it and then lifted out leaves a smooth stiff peak that holds its shape in the icing. (If the mixture is too soft, the peak will curl back; if too much icing sugar has been added, the peak will break off.)

If the icing is too stiff, dip a spatula into it and coat it thinly, then dip the spatula into strained, beaten egg white. Mix this into the icing, repeating the procedure until the correct consistency is reached.

Royal icing should be snow-white in colour. (If it is not mixed correctly, it will look slightly creamy.) To make royal icing even brighter, dip the tip of the brush handle into blue colouring and mix the colouring into the icing.

Royal icing for filigree work should not be stored for any length of time, but used on the day it is made. Mix small batches for immediate use, halving the quantities of ingredients given in the recipe. Be extra careful to get the consistency right; if the mixture is too stiff, the fine piped lines will not stick to each other and if it is too soft, the lines will spread.

Do not

☐ sift the icing sugar too long before mixing it with the egg white, as lumps may form;
☐ use an electric beater to make the icing, as too much air will be incorporated – burst air bubbles mar the appearance of the piping.

Hint: Here's a way to ensure that the icing sugar is fine and lump-free. Stretch a piece of silk or nylon cloth over a small glass or plastic jar and spoon 15 ml (3 teaspoons) of icing sugar on to it. Seal with a tight-fitting lid and shake the container vigorously.

Remove the lid carefully, keeping the cloth taut to prevent it slipping into the jar. Pour the sifted icing sugar into a clean, dry container and shake off the grains clinging to the cloth into another bowl. Take care not to mix up the two.

Repeat until you have enough sifted icing sugar. (Keep leftover grains for making butter icing.)

Guide-lines

The secret to successful filigree and lacework lies in practice and careful but confident handling of completed pieces. Make two or three times as many pieces as you need for the cake; if you know you have enough spares, you will feel less anxious about assembling them and will probably not break any!

The first step is to draw the pattern on a piece of paper (see *diagrams 50 to 73*, pages 61 to 69, for examples). When making original designs, remember to incorporate enough supporting lines, i.e. avoid long unconnected lines and introduce scrolls and coils with as many points of contact as possible.

Grease a metal disc or a piece of glass lightly with vegetable fat or white margarine. Place the pattern on top, grease and cover it with a piece of wax paper (you may use plastic instead, but then do not grease the pattern). Grease the wax paper or plastic too; a very thin layer that cannot be scraped off or absorbed by the piped icing (this will result in breakage).

Secure the greased wax paper or plastic with sticky tape to prevent its moving during piping.

Using a No. 00 tube and royal icing, first pipe the trellis lines, then the lines that will join them together, taking care to connect *all* the trellis and connecting lines. Using a No. 0 tube, complete the decorative parts of the design, ending with the short supporting curved or straight lines. Over-pipe where necessary.

Leave to dry completely.

The most difficult part of filigree work is removing the piped design from the wax paper or plastic. There are various methods, but all require practice and experience.

Using wax paper

☐ Place the metal disc, piping and all, in a moderately warm oven to melt the fat. Test with a fine brush: as soon as you can move the piped work, remove the disc carefully from the oven and place it on a flat surface. Slide a thin, firm strip of paper very carefully underneath the fili-

gree work, from one side to the other, until the whole piece is on the paper. Keep the paper flat as you move it along and *do not lift it*. Or:
☐ Melt the fat in a moderately warm oven as described above. Place a thin strip of sponge over the piped filigree work, slip one hand under the disc and, supporting the icing with your other hand, carefully turn it over so that the piping lies face down on the sponge. Remove the metal disc, then strip off the wax paper *very* carefully. Or:
☐ Remove the piping and disc from the oven once the fat has melted and place it on a table. Loosen the wax paper, grip one end firmly and slide it off the disc, with the piping. Move it to the table edge so that the piping protrudes slightly. Slip the fingertips of one hand between the wax paper and filigree work and, supporting the icing with this hand, slowly pull the paper down with the other to separate the two and end up with the icing on the supporting hand. This method is for those who like to live dangerously – if you do, wear medical gloves to prevent dampness on your hands damaging the icing.

Using plastic

☐ This method does not require heating. Simply loosen the plastic with the piped design from the metal disc, place it face down on a piece of sponge and gently peel off the plastic, leaving the design on the sponge.

Before assembling the pieces on the cake, over-pipe the lines that join the various sections together. Remember to take hold of the pieces where they are at their most solid to avoid breaking the filigree. You could also use the handle of a thin paintbrush, as shown in *plate 3*.

Free-hand filigree and lacework can also be done on net nails (see *diagram 1* on page 12).

Plate 3
Handling filigree work with a paintbrush

Dia. 1
Net nails and metal
plates for filigree and
lacework

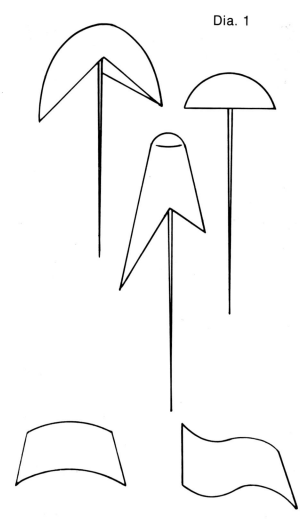

Plate 4
Progressives of built-
up line work

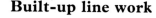

lengthening each line on either end by about 2 mm. Add an extra line on either side, piping five lines in all. Repeat right around the cake. Do the same in both diagonal directions, ending up with six layers of lines.

☐ *Note:* Ensure that each line is exactly in line with the one beneath it, otherwise you will lose the grid effect.

☐ Continue lengthening and adding on lines until the pattern spaces have been completely filled (see *plate 4*).

☐ When piping *ovals*, lengthen the two sets of diagonal lines by 3 to 4 mm, and the vertical lines by 2 mm. If you do not do this, you will end up with a round instead of an oval dome.

☐ *Note:* Pipe the first five sets of lines with tube No. 0 and the rest with tube No. 00.

Built-up line work

Built-up line work is done directly on to the cake using Nos. 0 and 00 tubes and royal icing.

☐ Prick out the design on the fondant (see *plate 4* for a pattern).

☐ Starting in the middle of a section, work from top to bottom: pipe three vertical lines approximately 2 mm apart, the middle one slightly longer than the other two. Repeat this piping in sections to match right around the cake.

☐ Return to the first three lines and pipe another three lines (the same length) over them, but this time diagonally from right to left (see *plate 4*). Repeat for other piped lines.

☐ The next step is to pipe three lines from left to right over the previous two sets of lines to obtain a grid with vertical and diagonal, but *no horizontal*, lines.

☐ Return to the first section again. Pipe a fourth set of lines in exactly the same position as the first set, i.e. running from top to bottom, but

Hollow linework

This is done on wax paper, left to dry and then attached to the cake with royal icing.

☐ Copy the design on to a sheet of paper (see *plate 5* for a pattern) and secure wax paper over it.

☐ Using a No. 0 tube and royal icing and starting at the wide end of the shape, pipe the first line following the outline of the pattern. Pipe a similar line on the opposite side, joining them neatly at the point. Allow to dry.

☐ Pipe a second line slightly off-centre over each

Plate 5
Progressives of piping
a hollow shape

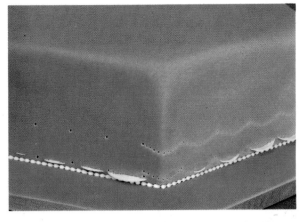
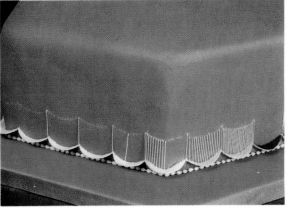

Plate 6
Progressives of
extension and bridge
work (the last three
steps indicate how *not*
to work)

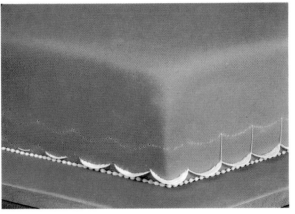
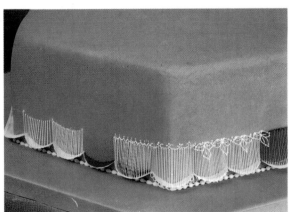

of the first, working towards the middle of the design. Allow to dry.

☐ Continue in this manner, shortening the lines time and again at the pointed end, until the built-up lines meet in the centre, forming an open-ended hollow shape (see *plate 5*).

☐ When dry, pipe a row of dots over the join in the centre and the edge of the open end to finish off the design.

☐ *Note:* If you do not let the lines dry before adding the next set, the whole structure will collapse.

Extension and bridge work

This technique, also known as "dropped string work" or "curtain borders", is a firm favourite, especially among Australian cake decorators.

Make sure that the extension work (see pattern in *plate 6*) never touches the cake board. It should be at least 4 mm above the board to prevent breakage should the board move.

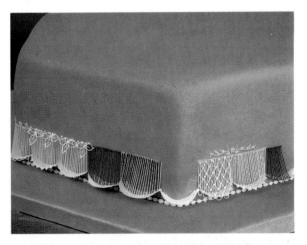

☐ To start, measure the circumference and height of the cake and cut a strip of wax paper accordingly, adding an extra 20 mm on one of the short sides to allow for overlapping.

☐ Fold the paper in half (two short sides meeting) and fold 10 mm back on either side. Fold

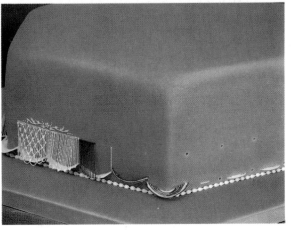

the whole in half again to obtain quarters. Successive folding will give you eighths, sixteenths, and so on. The design will dictate how many folds you will need.

☐ Draw a row of scallops 4 mm above the bottom edge of the folded wax paper, then draw a similar row of scallops above them. You could add a straight line instead of this second row of scallops. The distance from the top row of scallops will depend on the depth of the cake – 50 mm is about the average distance between the top scallops/straight line and those at the bottom. Exert sufficient pressure when drawing to ensure that, when unfolded, the design will be clearly visible along the entire length of paper.

☐ Fold the wax paper around the cake and secure it with adhesive tape where the two 10 mm strips overlap. Secure further by pressing pins into the points where the top scallops meet or, in the case of a straight line, at regular short intervals.

☐ Prick the top and bottom lines out on to the cake, making sure that all the details have come through, for once the pattern has been removed, it is impossible to reposition it exactly over the original placing. Pull out the pins and remove the paper carefully.

☐ Pipe beading, a snail's trail or small shell designs around the cake, below the lower edge of the pricked-out design. Pretty small shells can be made using Country Kitchen tubes, or Ateco tubes Nos. 13, 14 or 16, or a No. 42 Bekenal tube. This border will ensure that the extension work will be 4 mm or more above the board.

☐ Using a No. 1, 0 or 00 tube and royal icing, begin piping the extension work in the *middle* of each bottom scallop: pipe a 10 mm line, moving around the cake until each scallop has this base line.

☐ When dry, follow the outline of the pricked-out design and pipe a second line that touches both the cake and the first line and extends from 2 mm on the left to 2 mm on the right of the first line.

☐ Continue piping in this manner until you reach the top of each scallop and they all meet at these corners (see *plate 6*).

☐ *Note:* Each following line should be piped in such a way that the completed extension work, viewed from the front, presents the piped lines as a *straight* solid base. This can be achieved by placing them exactly in line as you work towards you. If placed off-centre, a cupped effect results. Also ensure that each line is at least partially dry before you apply the next one. If you work too quickly, the built-out scallop will either sag or collapse.

☐ Six to nine piped lines in total are needed.

☐ A bigger tube (No. 2 or 3) can be used to do extension work, but the result will not be as delicate.

☐ *Hint:* Extension work can be finished off by flooding. Colour the royal icing to match the cake and the other decorations.

After completion, allow the extension work to dry completely, then do the bridge work:

Follow the recipe for royal icing given on page 10 (ingredients based on 1 egg white).

A No. 0 or 00 tube is generally used for bridge work, although experienced decorators could reach for an injection needle secured in the nose of an icing tube. Bridge work requires precision and a steady hand. It is hard on the eyes, so do not work at it for longer than 30 to 60 minutes at a time. Take a break every so often to lessen the strain on your eyes and rest your hand.

☐ The top straight or scalloped line of the pattern serves as your guide. To start, pipe two vertical lines from the top of the design to the points on either side of a built-out scallop below.

☐ Pipe a third line, reaching to the tip of the scallop, in the middle of the space formed by the first two lines. This is how you do it: place the tube on the top line of the design and, squeezing the icing bag, gradually move the nozzle down towards the extension work. For a neat finish, bring the tube over and around the edge to end underneath the built-out scallop.

☐ Fill in the lefthand space with piped lines, leaving sufficient space between them for another line. Do the same in the righthand space (see *plate 6*).

☐ Repeat this procedure right around the cake and, when dry, fill the spaces with "dropped strings".

This method not only ensures that you can space lines evenly, but also enables you to remove broken or faulty lines relatively easily, using a paintbrush.

Finish off the top straight or scalloped line of the design with scrolls, beading or previously made lace points. Complete the bridge work with dots, over-piping or dropped lacework (see *plate*).

Double the bridge work by extending the built-up scallops (in the same way as they were originally formed) and piping strings from the top of the design, over the first set of strings, to the edge of the newly-formed extension (see *plate 6*). Using a darker or contrasting colour for the innermost set of bridges is particularly effective.

Modelling paste

As the name implies, this paste is used for moulding flowers and other decorations (see pages 17 to 36). Two recipes are given; the first is recommended for use in winter-rainfall areas or regions where the humidity is high.

Recipe 1

25 ml (5 t) cold water
10 ml (2 t) gelatine
15 ml (1 T) white vegetable fat (15 g)
800 ml (14 oz) sifted icing sugar (400 g)
25 ml (5 t) gum tragacanth or CMC
35 ml (7 t) egg white (1 large egg), strained through a muslin cloth and beaten until white and frothy

☐ Place the 25 ml (5 t) cold water in a small bowl; sprinkle the gelatine over and allow it to soak.
☐ Grease a large glass bowl with some of the fat and suspend it over a saucepan of hot water (the bottom of the bowl should not touch the water). Place half the icing sugar in the bowl, add the gum tragacanth or CMC and stir. Transfer to the stove and bring the water to the boil. Leave for about 10 minutes to heat the icing sugar (take care not to overheat it).
☐ Melt the soaked gelatine over hot water.
☐ Remove the bowl from the saucepan. Make a well in the icing sugar and add the gelatine and beaten egg white. *Beat well until the mixture becomes white and sticky.* This is very important, as the mixture would otherwise be too soft and not white enough.
☐ Add the rest of the icing sugar and mix well. The paste will have a fairly stiff consistency.
☐ Rub some of the remaining fat on your hands and knead the icing mixture until it is quite cold. Form into a smooth ball. Rub fat all over the ball, place it in a plastic bag and seal it in an airtight container.
☐ Refrigerate for at least 12 hours.
☐ Cut walnut-sized pieces from the hard stiff modelling paste. Grease your hands with a little fat and knead the pieces of paste until soft and pliable. Repeat until all the paste has been worked in this way, gradually combining the pieces to form one big ball again.
☐ Grease the ball with fat, place it in the plastic bag and refrigerate it in the airtight container until required.
☐ The ball of paste should be kneaded at least once a week while being stored.

Microwave method for recipe 1 (with kind permission from Jeanette van Niekerk)
☐ Place half the icing sugar and all the gum tragacanth in a greased glass bowl. Microwave on full power for 50 seconds, remove from the oven and stir well. Repeat twice more.
☐ Microwave the soaked gelatine for 16 seconds on full power, or until clear.
☐ Follow the instructions for Recipe 1.

Note:
15 ml (1 T) Tylose C 1000 P may be used instead of 25 ml (5 t) gum tragacanth or CMC, but an extra 125 ml (2 oz) (60 g) icing sugar will have to be added.

Recipe 2

10 ml (2 t) gelatine powder
25 ml (5 t) cold water
900 ml (1 lb) sifted icing sugar (450 g)
15 ml (1 T) gum tragacanth or CMC
10 ml (2 t) liquid glucose
15 ml (1 T) white vegetable fat (15 g)
45 ml (3 T) egg white (1 extra-large egg, plus 5 - 10 ml (1 - 2 t) more)

☐ Soak the gelatine in the cold water.
☐ Sift half the icing sugar and all the gum tragacanth or CMC into a well-greased glass bowl. Place over a saucepan of boiling water and heat for approximately 10 minutes, taking care not to overheat the mixture.
☐ In the meantime, dissolve the gelatine over hot water. Add the liquid glucose and vegetable fat and heat until melted.
☐ Make a well in the centre of the icing sugar. Add the egg white and gelatine mixture and stir until well-incorporated.
☐ Remove the bowl from the saucepan of boiling water and beat the mixture with a wooden spoon until quite white and sticky. Insufficient beating will result in a too-soft, off-white paste.
☐ Add the rest of the icing sugar. Grease your hands with vegetable fat and knead the mixture thoroughly.
☐ Grease the ball of paste with vegetable fat and place it in a plastic bag in an airtight container. Refrigerate for 12 to 24 hours.
☐ See Recipe 1 for the remaining kneading instructions.

Note:
☐ Do not add the glucose and fat to the gelatine before it has dissolved completely, as grey specks may otherwise form in the modelling paste.
☐ If the paste is too hard when you want to use it, knead in small quantities of egg white to make it more pliable.

Plate 7
Birthday cake for a music lover. The violin and sheet music were made from pastillage (see *patterns 80 to 83*). The floral arrangement consists of tiger lilies and shoots of the variegated periwinkle (see pages 34 to 36 for detailed descriptions). The side of the cake is finished off with embroidery work (see *diagram 110*)

Pastillage

Pastillage differs from modelling paste in that it is not moulded but rolled out and cut into shapes according to various patterns. It is used to make objects such as plaques, birthday cards, baskets, musical instruments, bells, and so on (see *plate 7*).

15 ml (1 T) gelatine (10 g)
60 ml (¼ c) cold water
10 ml (2 t) liquid glucose
5 ml (1 t) cream of tartar, dissolved in 10 ml cold water
500 - 750 ml (2 - 3 c) sifted icing sugar (250 - 380 g)
250 ml (1 c) cornflour (120 g)

☐ Soak the gelatine in the cold water, then melt it over hot water.
☐ Add the liquid glucose and cream of tartar solution. Stir until well-mixed.
☐ Place half the icing sugar and all the cornflour in a large mixing bowl. Add the liquid and beat until the mixture becomes sticky.
☐ Pour into an airtight container and store in the refrigerator.

When needed, take the required quantity of mixture and add enough of the remaining sifted icing sugar to it to form a paste that does not stick to the hands. Roll out and cut (see *diagrams 80 to 85*, pages 74 to 76, for examples of patterns).

Place a copy of the pattern underneath a piece of glass and secure it. Sprinkle the top of the glass with cornflour and arrange the cut-out pastillage on it to correspond with the pattern below. Leave to dry. Turn the pastillage over after several hours to allow the reverse to dry.

Repeat the turning over process several times to prevent the pieces warping. When set, place on a piece of thick sponge to dry completely.

Flood icing

The base for flood icing is royal icing (see recipe on page 10, *but do not mix in the glucose and gum*). Using cold water or egg white, thin a little royal icing (depending on the size of the area to be flooded). To check consistency, cut a line through the mixture with the sharp edge of a knife. In warm dry weather the cut should close up by the count of seven, and in cold and/or wet conditions by the count of ten.

If you are not familiar with the technique of flooding, consult the first *Sugar art* book in this series. (See also *diagrams 86 to 98*, pages 77 to 87 in this book, for examples of patterns.)

Flowers, ferns and fillers

Agapanthus

This species carries magnificent umbels of blue or white flowers and has long, smooth strap-shaped leaves. A single head can consist of up to 200 blooms. The stems are smooth and vary from 60 cm to 120 cm in length.

The instructions that follow are for making buds and blooms as these, not the umbels, are used for cake decorating.

Making the bud
☐ You require a ball of white modelling paste, about 8 mm in diameter, and a length of wire (gauge 26).
☐ Shape the paste into a teardrop over one end of the wire. It should be about 30 mm long and 7 mm wide across the widest part.
☐ Pinch the bulge so that the "teardrop" is pointed at the top (see *diagram 2*).
☐ Use a scalpel or a sharp knife to make five incisions down the length of the bud. This marks the base of the petals.
☐ Paint the tip and the base pale green.

Making the bloom
☐ To start off with, you need a length of 26 gauge wire, six white stamens (17 mm to 22 mm in length, plus an additional 10 mm to allow for taping down) and a pistil, 27 mm plus 10 mm long (to make the pistil, merely cut the anther off a seventh stamen).
☐ Paint the anthers pale ochre.
☐ Tape the stamens and pistil to the wire and bend them at an angle of 45°, curving their tips back and upwards as shown in *diagram 3A*.
☐ Form a ball of white paste into a Mexican hat shape (the crown should not be more than 8 mm high). Roll out the "rim" thinly and cut out, using a template or cutter made according to the measurements of *diagram 4* (see also *diagram 3B*).
☐ Place the flower, face down, on the palm of your hand and roll out the edges of the petals with a ball tool, thinning them but not changing their shape.
☐ Turn over and cup each petal with the ball tool.

☐ Push a 10 mm dowel stick, sharpened like a pencil, into the tube of the flower to hollow it out. Before removing the dowel, bend the petals down towards it to form a trumpet-shaped flower (see *diagram 3C*).
☐ Make incisions from the corners where the petals meet nearly to the base of the tube (see *diagram 3D*).
☐ Using a veining tool or a hat-pin, draw lines up the centre of each petal from base to tip to form the midribs or principal veins (see *diagram 3E*).

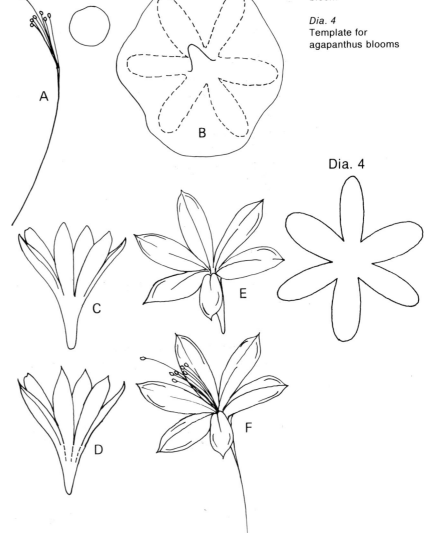

Dia. 2
Making an agapanthus bud

Dia. 3
Making an agapanthus bloom

Dia. 4
Template for agapanthus blooms

☐ Leave the flower hanging over the dowel stick for a few minutes to allow the paste to set.

☐ Insert the stamens and pistil by pushing the wire right through the centre of the tube. Secure at the base with egg white. (They should be placed to one side in the flower, with their tips curled back – see *diagram 3F*.)

☐ When completely dry, dust the heart of the flower yellow-green using powder colouring. Dust the tips of the petals and the base of the tube outside.

☐ Agapanthus blooms can be used either on their own or combined with other flowers such as small roses, carnations and gypsophila. They are particularly effective in corsages or bridal bouquets (see *plate 8*).

Plate 8
Buds, half-open and open blooms of the agapanthus (see white flowers)

Peruvian lily
(*Alstroemeria aurantiaca*)

These showy, irregularly shaped flowers vary in colour from bright orange to various shades of red, depending on variety or cultivar. A single flower consists of six perianth segments, i.e. three large and three smaller petals arranged around six stamens and a pistil with a three-parted stigma.

Making the pistil

☐ Cover a piece of 32 gauge wire, about 50 mm in length, with a quarter width of white tape (You could use fuse wire instead.) Cut the tape off 20 mm above the end of the covered wire and divide this lengthwise into three equal strips (see *diagrams 5A and 5B*).

☐ Twist each strip between the thumb and forefinger to form three "feelers". Cut each strip back to about 3 mm long and curve it downwards (see *diagram 5C*).

☐ Paint the whole pistil pink, using vegetable colouring (see note under stamens below).

Making the stamens

☐ Use artificial stamens of the same length as that used for the pistil and attach a tiny ball of grey paste (about 1 mm in diameter) to one end. Make six.

☐ Paint the stamens pink using vegetable colouring (*note* that adjustments are necessary when varieties or cultivars other than shown in *plate 9* are made).

☐ Tape the pistil and stamens to a length of 26 gauge wire, ensuring that the completed pistil is about 35 mm and the stamens 30 mm long (see *diagram 5D*).

Making the petals

☐ Roll a ball of white paste into a sausage shape (the colour will have to be adjusted according to variety or cultivar) (see *diagram 6A*).

☐ Flatten the paste with a roller, first to the one side and then to the other, leaving a small ridge at the base in the middle of the paste (see *diagram 6B*).

☐ Cut out a narrow petal (see *diagram 9* on page 20 for size and shape of template) and thin the edges with a ball tool (see *diagram 6C*).

☐ Turn the petal over and draw a short vein, about 5 mm long, from the tip down the centre. Turn it over again and pinch the tip of the petal lightly to emphasize the newly formed vein (see *diagram 6D*). Cup the area left and right of this, at the back, using a ball tool.

☐ Apply egg white to one end of a piece of 32 gauge wire (fuse wire could also be used) and in-

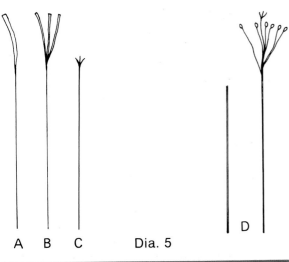

A   B   C   Dia. 5   D

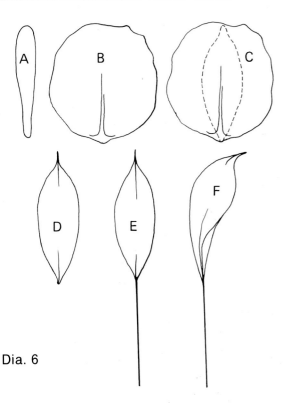

A   B   C

D   E   F

Dia. 6

sert it about 10 mm deep in the base of the petal (see *diagram 6E*). Secure firmly.

☐ Curve the tip of the petal slightly backwards and pinch the base at the back to form a small groove in front (see *diagram 6F*).

☐ Place the petal over the back of a teaspoon to maintain the curved shape and allow to dry completely.

☐ Make two more petals.

☐ Follow the first two steps of these instructions and cut out the larger petal (see *diagram 10* on page 20 for a template; see also *diagrams 7A and 7B*). Thin the edges with a ball tool.

☐ Pinch the tip of the petal at the back and, while holding it here, form an indentation down the centre of the front, using the flat end of a veining tool (see *diagram 7C*).

☐ Turn the petal over and cup it on either side so that the edges curl back slightly.

☐ Following the instructions given for the first set of petals, insert a piece of wire at the base (see *diagram 7D*). Pinch to form a groove.

☐ Leave the first 10 mm of the base straight and curve the rest of the petal back at an angle (see *diagram 7E*).

☐ Rest the top part on a piece of polyurethane and allow the petal to dry.

☐ Make two more petals.

☐ Dust the front and back of the narrow petals with pale pink colouring powder and shade with

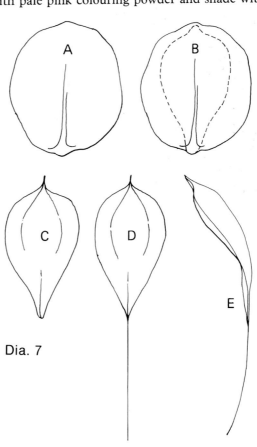

A   B

C   D

E

Dia. 7

Dia. 5
Peruvian lily: making the pistil and stamens

Dia. 6
Peruvian lily: making the small petal

Dia. 7
Peruvian lily: making the large petal

Plate 9
Peruvian lilies

19

green powder. The tips should be a fairly bright green.

☐ Paint elongated lengthwise maroon flecks on the front over the whole petal (see *plate 9*).

☐ Dust the larger petals in a similar fashion on the front. Turn the petal over and paint a filled-in area similar to the shape of a narrow petal, stretching over the bulge to the tip. Paint the hollow areas on either side pale pink.

Assembling the flower

☐ Apply egg white to the base of the pistil and stamens, and attach a small ball of white paste, about 2 mm in diameter.

☐ Tape the three smaller petals around the stamens to the stem: place two overlapping each other on one side and the remaining one opposite them (see *diagram 8A*). (This will leave two spaces, one to the left and one to the right of the single petal.)

☐ Arrange two of the larger petals, opposite each other, in these spaces and place the third one behind the overlapping narrow petals (see *diagram 8B*). Tape to the stem.

☐ Mould a ball of green paste of about 5 mm in diameter around the base of the petals to form the ovary. Taper it at the bottom and make incisions in the thicker part to form three sections. Smooth the edges of these sections over the petals using the flat end of a veining tool (there should be no ridge).

Hint: Instead of stem leaves, use fern fronds with Peruvian lilies (see page 30 for instructions).

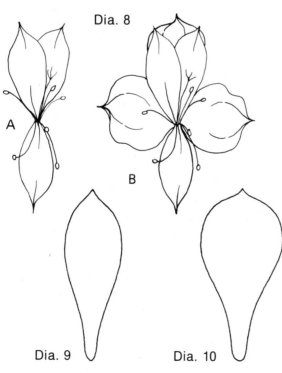

Dia. 8

A

B

Dia. 9   Dia. 10

Dia. 8
Peruvian lily: assembling the pistil, stamens and petals

Dia. 9
Peruvian lily: template for small petals

Dia. 10
Peruvian lily: template for large petals

Azalea *(Rhododendron)*

There are a large number of *Rhododendron* species, differing in size, colour and shape of petals. Some are plain coloured throughout, whilst others have spots on the three upper petals. The petals vary in shape from elongated to rounded, but are always attached to a short trumpet – they are never singly arranged in a calyx.

Making the stamens and pistil

☐ Once assembled, the pistil is about 30 mm and the stamens 15 to 20 mm in length. Add 15 mm to each to allow for taping.

☐ Cover a piece of 24 gauge wire, about 70 mm long, with green florist's tape and tape seven artificial stamens and a pistil to it (see *diagram 11*).

☐ Colour the anthers light brown to pink and the stamens pink (check your model flower for colouring). Attach a small ball of yellow paste, about 2 mm in diameter, to the tip of the pistil to form the stigma. Flatten it on top and make a shallow incision across it.

Making the flower

☐ Use paste coloured according to your model flower. To obtain a pearly shade, use white paste and paint the petals once completed. Roll a piece of paste into a cone, about 25 mm long and 15 mm wide across the base. Flatten the paste around the edge to form a shape similar to that of a Mexican hat (see *diagram 12A*).

☐ Cut out the flower using a five-petal cutter about 46 mm in diameter (see *diagram 12B*). Lift the paste and press the sharp point of an Anger tool into the centre of the flower to form a trumpet. Lay the flower, with the tool still in it, flat on the work surface and roll the tool backwards and forwards to hollow out the trumpet and flatten one petal. Lift and turn the paste anti-clockwise, rolling the tool as described, until all the petals have been flattened (see *diagram 12C*).

☐ Place the flower on the work surface with the petals face down and make 5 mm cuts up the trumpet, in the corners where the petals meet (see *diagram 12D*).

☐ Choose one of the petals as the main one and curl back the two petals on either side of it. Lift the flower by its trumpet and flatten the edges of the main petal so that it overlaps the other two at the base (their upper edges must lie *behind* the base edges of the main petal). Ruffle the edge of the main petal right around with an Anger tool (see *diagram 12E*).

☐ Flatten and ruffle the edges of the adjacent petals in the same way, maintaining the initial overlaps and forming new overlaps with the re-

Dia. 11
Azalea: making
stamens and a pistil

Dia. 12
Azalea: making the
flower and calyx

maining two petals (their upper edges should lie *behind* the lower edges of petals two and three) (see *diagram 12F*).

☐ Flatten and ruffle these petals as well, allowing the base of the one on the right to overlap the front of the other.

☐ Using a veining tool, make principal veins in the centre of each petal.

☐ Apply egg white to the base of the stamens where they meet the stem, insert it into the flower and secure by moulding the paste of the trumpet around it (see *diagram 12G*).

Making the calyx

☐ Mould a small ball of green paste (about 5 mm in diameter) into the shape of a Mexican hat (see *diagram 12H*).

☐ Cut out the calyx with a five-leaved calyx cutter about 12 mm in diameter (see *diagram 12I*).

☐ Thin each sepal to measure about 5 mm and insert the sharp point of an Anger tool into the heart of the calyx to form a trumpet. When completed, the calyx should measure about 10 mm from tip of sepal to end of trumpet (see *diagram 12J*).

Assembling the flower and finishing it off

☐ Apply egg white to the inner wall of the calyx trumpet and insert the flower, with stamens and pistil, pushing the stem right through so that the calyx hugs the base of the flower. Curl the sepals back.

☐ The azaleas in *plate 10* were made with white paste, then coloured with pale pink powder colouring. The edges of the petals are left white and the shading becomes deeper towards the heart of the flower. Shade similarly on reverse side.

Making buds

☐ Follow the instructions under "Making the flower", but fold the petals over each other, crinkling them slightly at the edges. When completed it resembles a rose bud.

☐ Dust with powder colouring.

☐ Add a calyx as for the flower.

Making the leaves

☐ The leaves are dark green on top and paler green underneath, and vary in length from 10 mm to 20 mm. They are arranged in groups around the bases of the flowers, (see *plate 10*).

☐ For detailed instructions, see page 28 under *Honeysuckle*, but use *diagram 13* as a template.

Assembling a cluster of flowers

☐ Tape together two flowers, a bud and as many stem leaves as required.

Dia. 13
Azalea: template for
stem leaves (make
smaller and larger
versions)

Dia. 13

Plate 10
An arrangement of
azaleas and baby's
breath

Baby's breath
(Gypsophila paniculata)

This delightful genus contains myriads of small white, frothy flowers. Cake decorators often take "poetic licence" and colour them to tone in with the overall colour scheme of the cake.

☐ Thin out a twig of dried baby's breath by cutting off some of the florets and sprigs.

☐ Mix a quantity of flood icing, but apply a count test of 8 to 9, irrespective of weather or climatic conditions (see page 16). Colour if preferred. Cover each floret on the thinned out twig with this icing, using a paintbrush. Allow to dry.

☐ You could also take the further liberty of attaching minute flowers to some of the flood icing buds (see *plate 10*). These could be forget-me-nots piped with royal icing and a No. o tube (see *Sugar art* of 1984, page 17), flattened with the tip of a finger, or made from modelling paste (roll out and cut out with a 3 mm floral cutter).

Note: Only small quantities of stubble are permissible for show purposes.

Broom *(Cytisus* species*)*

They have wiry green stems, studded with tiny leaves and myriads of small pea-shaped flowers.

Making buds

☐ Cover a piece of 32 gauge wire, about 30 mm long, with green florist's tape (you could also use fuse wire).

☐ Mould a small ball of lemon-coloured paste into a cone. Depending on the size of bud you wish to make, it could range from 2 mm to 10 mm in length.

☐ Insert the covered wire into it and shape the cone to form a bud as shown in *diagram 14A*.

Making an half-open flower

☐ Roll out a piece of lemon paste very thinly and cut out (see *diagram 17* for template; see also *diagram 14B*). Place, face down, on the palm of your hand and pinch from tip to base to form a midrib (see *diagram 14C*).

☐ Fold around a large bud as shown in *diagram 14D*, securing them with egg white.

☐ Pinch the tip of the petal slightly and curl it back so that the sides gape open, exposing the bud inside (see *diagram 14E*).

Making the flower

☐ Roll out a piece of lemon paste very thinly and cut out a petal (see *diagram 17* for template; see also *diagram 14F*).

☐ Slit the petal down the centre from the wide end to the base, leaving about 5 mm intact (see *diagram 14G*).

☐ Place, face upwards, on the palm of your hand and roll out with a ball tool to cup and curl the petal edge on either side (see *diagram 14H*).

☐ Fold around a large bud, securing it with egg white at the base, being the pointed end (see *diagram 14I* for shape and position of the two parts).

☐ Holding the flower in one hand, grip the two tips on either side of the slit and push them down towards the base to let the petal balloon around the bud. Allow to dry.

☐ Roll and cut out a second petal (see *diagram 14J*). Place, face down, on the palm of your hand and pinch from tip to base to form a midrib (see *diagram 14K*). Roll out the paste with a ball tool on either side of the rib to cup the petal. The base is now the rounded end (see *diagram 14L*).

☐ Apply egg white to the base of the puffed petal and attach the newly formed one as shown in *diagram 14M*. Grip at the tip and curl back, forming an angle of about 90° between the two.

Making the calyx

☐ Roll out a piece of green paste very thinly and cut out the calyx, using a small rose-petal cutter about 9 mm from tip to base (see *diagram 15A*).

☐ Attach with egg white to the bases of buds and flowers as shown in *diagrams 15B and 15C*.

Assembling a spray of flowers and buds

☐ Tape together at 5 mm intervals a collection of the smallest buds.

☐ Attach a length of 22 gauge wire just below the last bud to serve as a stem. Tape another collection of buds to it, enlarging the buds and increasing the spaces between them as you work

Dia. 14

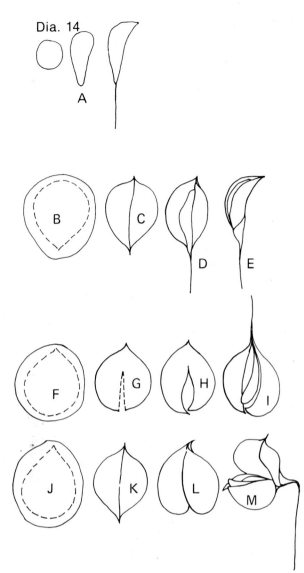

Dia. 15

Plate 11
Buds, half-open and open blooms of the broom (see yellow flowers)

Dia. 14
Broom: making a bud, half-open and open flower

Dia. 15
Broom: making a calyx

Dia. 16
Broom: assembling flowers and buds into a raceme

☐ The five stamens and pistil of these flowers only become visible once they start dying off. They protrude at the tip and curve back towards the stem, ranging from 6 mm to 2 mm in length from top to bottom. The pistil measures about 10 mm.

Note:
☐ The sprays could be slim, consisting of a variety of buds only, or they could be short and contain a cluster of open flowers. This allows scope as far as your arrangements are concerned.
☐ Stem leaves are not necessary for sprays of broom.

Flame-lily *(Gloriosa superba)*

A gem of a flower consisting of six deep, rich orange or red petals, shaded yellow towards the heart. The six stamens and the pistil are borne below the corolla.

Making the stamens
☐ Cover an 80 mm piece of 32 gauge wire (or fuse wire) with green florist's tape. Bend the wire at a right angle 15 mm below the top end and fold it back on itself to form a "T", measuring 5 mm on either side, with the vertical length of wire (see *diagrams 18A and 18B*). Twist the doubled piece into one (see *diagrams 18C and 18D*).
☐ Fold a ball of yellow paste, about 3 mm in diameter, over the crossbar to cover it completely (see *diagrams 18E and 18F*). Cut away the paste at the bottom as shown in *diagram 18G* to obtain an anther about 9 mm wide and 2 mm high. Hold the anther between your thumb and index finger and make a lengthwise incision from end to end (see *diagram 18H*). Paint the slit with green colouring.

Dia. 16

Dia. 17
Broom: template for half-open and open flowers

Dia. 17

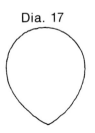

your way down. End with the largest bud reaching about halfway up the calyx of the bud just above it (when they are both held flush with the stem).
☐ Add a few half-open flowers and finally some fully opened flowers (see *diagram 16*).
☐ Note that all the flowers and buds should be arranged with their backs towards the stem (see *plate 11*).
☐ Paint the smallest buds a greeny brown. Gradually shade to green, then green with yellow tips as the buds get bigger, ending with the largest ones left the lemon colour of the paste.

23

Dia. 18
Flame-lily: making
stamens, a pistil and
petals

Dia. 18

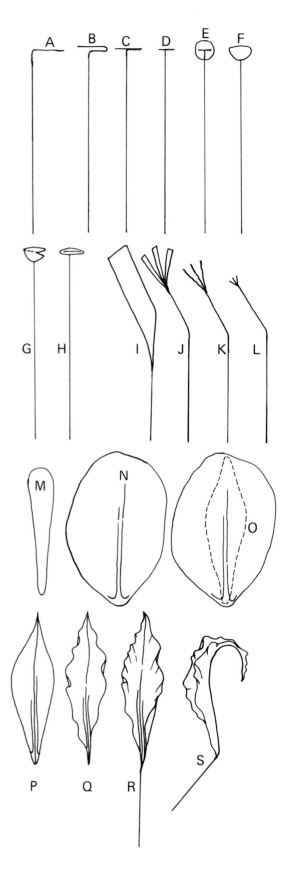

Making the pistil

☐ Cover a 150 mm piece of 20 gauge wire with green florist's tape (full width) (see *diagram 18I*). Do not cut the tape off but continue rolling it into a tight spiral until about 20 mm in length. Cut it off straight 10 mm beyond the end of the spiral and divide into three equal strips (see *diagram 18J*). Twist between your fingers to form a three-parted stigma (see *diagram 18K*). Cut each back to 4 mm long (see *diagram 18L*).

Making the petals

☐ Roll a piece of yellow paste into a cone 50 mm long, 8 mm wide at the base and 3 mm wide across the tip (see *diagram 18M*).

☐ Roll out the paste to the left and the right, leaving in the centre a ridge that tapers from base to tip. Cut out a petal (see *diagram 23* on p. 26 for template; see also *diagram 18O*) and draw a principal vein down its centre, over the bulge. Turn the petal over and pinch the paste from tip to base to form a midrib at the back (see *diagram 18P*).

☐ Ruffle the edges of the petal with a toothpick or a similar small tool (see *diagram 18Q*).

☐ Turn the petal over and run over the principal vein *in front*, using a veining tool.

☐ Cover a 30 mm length of wire (gauge 32) with green or white florist's tape and insert it 10 mm deep into the base of the petal. Grip the wire about 15 mm higher between your thumb and index finger and flatten the lower 5 mm of paste to form a "waist" (see *diagram 18R*).

☐ At the base of the petal, bend the wire at right angles and then curl the petal as shown in *diagram 18S* to form a "question mark". Lay it down on its side and allow to dry.

☐ Make two more petals, then three that are slightly narrower.

☐ Paint a red "V" on the face of each petal, the tip reaching down 15 mm above the base and the points on either side to 30 mm above it. Leave the remainder of the surface yellow (see *diagram 19A*). Turn the petal over and paint red markings on either side of the rib. Leave a thin yellow line in the centre and an unpainted yellow crescent shape, 25 mm long and 5 mm wide in the centre, left and right of the vein (see *diagram 19B*).

☐ Roll a small ball of green paste, about 2 mm in diameter, into a sausage about 1 mm in diameter and 10 mm in length. Shape the ends into points. Cut in half crosswise to obtain two small cones.

☐ Attach one of the cones to the base of a petal with egg white. The tip should face upwards (see *diagram 20*). Pinch the paste down the centre to form a triangular sepal with a midrib. Paint the midrib with white colouring.

24

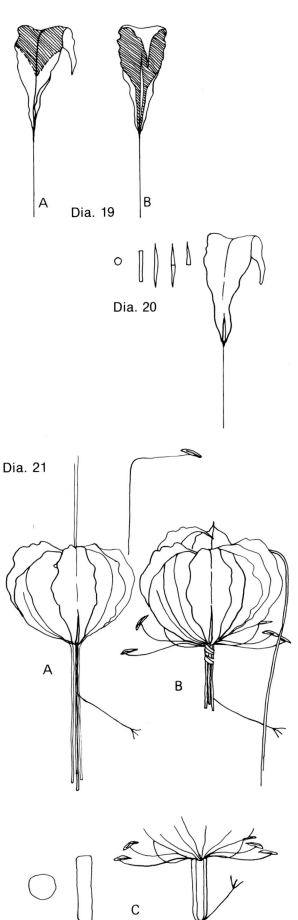

□ Paint a thin green line, about 25 mm long, down the rib of the petal at the back. Paint green colouring over the red layer at the base, covering an area of 5 mm.

Assembling the flower

□ Hold the stem upright with the pistil end downwards. Tape the three narrow petals trigonally around it, about 15 mm from the corner where the pistil and stem meet. The tips of the petals should curl inwards towards the stem, as shown in *diagram 21A*.

□ Arrange the remaining petals in the spaces left between these petals and cut off the wires so that they end where the pistil begins.

□ Bend the lower 30 mm of each stamen down and tape it to the 15 mm of stem between the bases of the flower and the pistil. Cut off the 15 mm excess wire. The stamens should be arranged in a circle, one opposite each of the petals (see *diagram 21B*).

□ Roll a ball of green paste, about 10 mm in diameter, into a sausage shape about 6 mm in diameter and 15 mm long. Flatten it slightly and fold it around the 15 mm section between the bases of the flower and pistil to cover all the wires. Make three equally spaced lengthwise incisions to form a three-lobed ovary. Smooth the paste at the bottom down the pistil, and up and between the petals (see *diagram 21C*).

□ Bend the pistil up towards the flower and curve the stamens. Turn the anthers parallel. Bend the stem (still vertical) near the heart of the flower to pass between two of the petals, and curve it as shown in *plate 12*.

Dia. 19
Flame-lily: how to paint the petals

Dia. 20
Flame-lily: finishing off a petal

Dia. 21
Assembling a flame-lily

Plate 12
Flame-lilies with broom, honeysuckle and baby's breath

Making the leaves

☐ Roll out green paste and cut out leaves (see *diagram 24* for template). Note that a fully grown leaf measures about 80 mm by 45 mm (across its widest part). The cross-measurement about 30 mm from the tip can be as narrow as 15 mm.

☐ Roll out the edges lightly to curve them and curl back the point of the leaf (see *diagram 22*).

☐ Draw a principal vein down the centre and a prominent one on either side of it (three in all). Exert enough pressure to ensure that three distinct ribs will be visible on the back of the leaf. Add a few less distinct lengthwise veins.

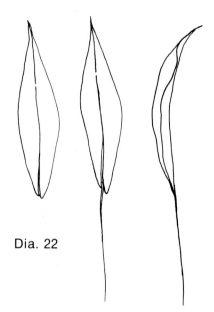

Dia. 22

Dia. 22
Flame-lily: making a stem leaf

Dia. 23
Flame-lily: template for petals

Dia. 24
Flame-lily: template for stem leaves (make smaller and larger versions)

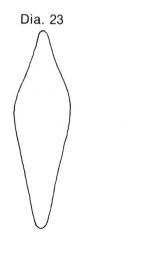 Dia. 23

 Dia. 24

Plate 13
A spray of fuchsias

Fuchsia

Fuchsias are tubular pendant flowers, in attractive shades of red, purple and pink. They have four short petals framed by four long coloured sepals, in shades that contrast with that of the flower.

Making the stamens and pistil

☐ Cut eight pink stamens 40 mm long.

☐ Pistil: Attach a small ball of paste, about 1 mm in diameter in a colour corresponding with that of the species, to a stamen 50 mm long.

☐ Tape the stamens and pistil to a piece of 26 gauge wire so that the stamens measure 25 mm and the pistil 35 mm (see *diagram 25A*).

Making the petals

☐ Roll out paste of the appropriate colour very thinly and cut out four petals (see *diagram 26* for template; see also *diagram 25B*).

☐ Thin the edges with a ball tool and cup the petals.

☐ Apply egg white to the base of each petal and place them on top of each other, fanning them out slightly at the top (see *diagram 25C*).

Assembling the flower

☐ Mould a small ball of paste, about 2 mm in diameter in the required colour, around the base of the stamens and pistil. Cover with egg white.

☐ Place the ball in the middle on the bottom edge of the fan of petals.

☐ Fold the petals from left to right around the stamens and pistil, enveloping the pistil and overlapping each other (see *plate 13* and *diagram 25D*).

☐ Allow to dry thoroughly.

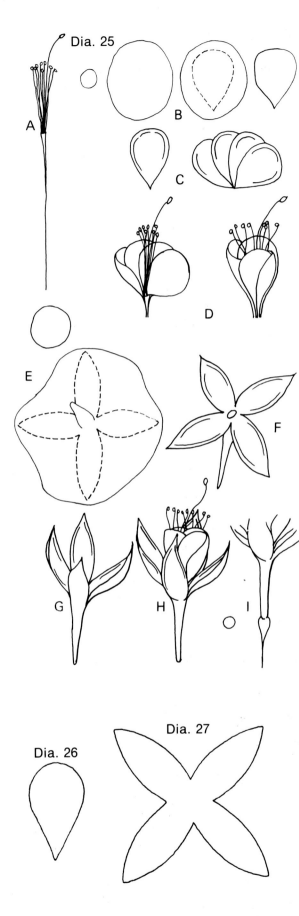

Dia. 25

Dia. 26

Dia. 27

Making the sepals

☐ Shape a ball of paste in the appropriate colour to the shape of a Mexican hat (see *diagram 25E*). The length will be determined by the species you have chosen to make, but the "crown" should not measure more than 6 mm in diameter at the base.

☐ Cut out shapes for the sepals (see *diagram 27* for template).

☐ Thin the edges with a ball tool and cup each sepal lengthwise (see *diagram 25F*).

☐ Form a trumpet by inserting an Anger tool down the centre of the "crown".

☐ Curl and bend the trumpet and sepals according to the fuchsia species you have chosen (see *diagram 25G*).

Assembling the flower and sepals

☐ Apply egg white to the inner wall of the trumpet of the sepals and insert the stem with the flower. Secure (see *diagram 25H*).

☐ Bend the sepals towards, or away from, the petals to represent various stages of opening.

☐ Taper the paste of the trumpet down the stem. Note that the shape and length varies from species to species.

☐ Mould a small ball of green paste, about 5 mm in diameter, around the base of the trumpet to form an ovary (see *diagram 25I*).

☐ Paint the face of the sepals to complement the petals, and shade the back and the trumpet with the same colour.

☐ Apply a touch of green to the tips of the sepals.

Making the leaves

☐ Roll out two pieces of green paste very thinly; one a dark green and the other a lighter shade. Cut out two leaves (see *diagram 28* for template).

☐ Place a piece of fuse wire or 32 gauge wire on the pale green leaf and place the dark green one on top. Roll over the edges with a ball tool to secure them firmly.

☐ Draw a principal vein down the centre on the face of the leaf, and a few small veins branching from it.

☐ Curve and shape the leaves to look natural.

☐ Make a number of leaves of varying sizes.

Honeysuckle (*Lonicera periclymenum*)

The honeysuckle has strong clasping stems and creamy flowers arranged in pairs down the stem, with two tiny leaves arranged at the base and a larger one just below them.

The flowers are irregular in shape, their petals

Dia. 25
Fuchsia: making stamens, a pistil, petals and sepals

Dia. 26
Fuchsia: template for petals

Dia. 27
Fuchsia: template for sepals

Dia. 28
Fuchsia: template for stem leaves (make smaller and larger versions)

Dia. 28

arranged in a group of four at the top with a single one at the bottom. They are joined at the base, forming a long, narrow tube.

The age of the flowers can be determined by their colour: when the petals are white, the anthers are ripe; as the anthers fade, the petals turn yellow and the stigmas become receptive.

☐ Tape five stamens, varying in length from 16 mm to 20 mm, and a pistil (a stamen about 30 mm long) to a piece of 26 or 28 gauge wire. The measurements refer to the length of the stamens and pistil *after* taping, so add an extra 15 mm to each.
☐ Colour the anthers pale brown and the stigma pale green.
☐ Bend and curve them as indicated in *diagram 29A*.

Dia. 29
Honeysuckle: making a flower

Dia. 30
Honeysuckle: template for stem leaves (make smaller and larger versions)

Making the flower
☐ Mould a ball of cream or white paste, about 8 mm in diameter, into a cone 30 mm long, 1 mm wide across the base and 5 mm wide across the tip. Cut off the bulge of the tip to obtain a flat top (see *diagram 29B*).
☐ Cut the paste at the flat top of the cone, using a pair of scissors, to form a lip 2 mm wide, 10 mm long and 1 mm thick (see *diagram 29C*).
☐ Hold the paste upright between your thumb and index finger, with the tip pointing downwards and the "lip" draped over your index finger. Roll out the "lip" with a ball tool, lengthening it to 20 mm (this becomes the single petal) (see *diagram 29D*).
☐ Still holding the cone upright, drape the paste opposite the rolled out "lip" over your index finger. Work it over with the ball tool as described above, ensuring that the paste measures 20 mm in length and 10 mm across the top edge (see *diagram 29E*).
☐ Hold the paste upright so that the first, single petal lies between your thumb and index finger. Hollow it out lengthwise with a toothpick.
☐ Draw three vertical lines, evenly spaced, over the broader petal to divide it into four. Make incisions 3 mm deep down these lines and cut the edges round to form scallops (see *diagram 29F*). Hollow out as for front petal.
☐ Insert a toothpick into the head of the cone and hollow it out to form the tube of the flower (see *diagram 29G*).
☐ Apply egg white to the base of the stamens and pistil, and insert this into the flower, with the anthers and stigma curling up towards the group of four petals (see *plate 14* and *diagram 29H*).
☐ The completed flower measures about 50 mm

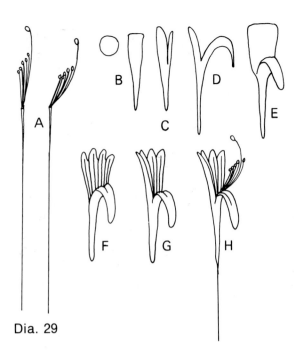

Dia. 29

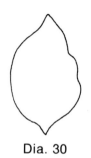

Dia. 30

from the tip of the highest petal to the base of the tube.

Making the stem leaves
☐ The leaves are almost heart-shaped (see *diagram 30* for template) and vary in length from about 8 mm x 5 mm to 30 mm x 15 mm.
☐ Roll out a piece each of dark green and pale green paste very thinly. Cut out.
☐ Apply egg white to a 30 mm piece of fuse wire or 32 gauge wire and lay it down the centre of the pale green leaf. Place the dark green leaf on top and press them together firmly.
☐ Use a real or artificial leaf to make a vein imprint on the dark green side.
☐ Roll out the edges lightly and curve them to look more natural.

Making the bud
☐ The buds vary in length from about 10 mm to approximately 30 mm. As they grow bigger, the colour changes from green to white with green tips.
☐ Roll white paste into a cone and insert fuse

wire or 32 gauge wire into it from the pointed end.

☐ Grip the paste on either side and push it together to form an upright, slightly bowed "S" (see *plate 14*).

☐ Use pale green colouring and paint the lower 1 mm of the tubes of the buds as well as the flowers.

Assembling a spray

☐ Tape buds to the top of a length of wire covered with green florist's tape, progressing to white and then yellow flowers, interspersed with leaves (see *plate 14*).

Lilac *(Syringa vulgaris)*

The flowers have four petals and are tubular, and the leaves are heart-shaped and smooth. Depending on cultivar, the lilac flower may be single or double and vary in colour from white to pale yellow, mauve, purple or reddish purple. For cake decorating purposes, they may be used individually as fillers, or arranged in sprays or clusters.

Making the flower

☐ Mould a small ball of white paste, about 6 mm in diameter, into the shape of a teardrop, measuring about 10 mm in length (see *diagram 31A*).

☐ Holding the bulge upwards, make an incision 5 mm deep and part the two halves. Split each into two (see *diagram 31B*) to obtain a circle of four sections. Spread them out evenly (see *diagram 31C*).

☐ Holding the paste upright, thin out each section over your index finger, using the flat part of a veining tool to obtain four petals.

☐ Pierce a hole in the heart of the flower with a pin and draw a principal vein from tip to base down the centre of each petal.

☐ Pinch the tips of the petals lightly to make them more pointed (see *diagram 31D*).

☐ Pull a small stamen through the hole until just its tip shows. Secure it at the base and smooth the paste (see *diagram 31E*).

Making buds

☐ Mould a "teardrop" over a stamen as described in step one under "Making the flower".

Make as many flowers and buds as required and assemble them as desired (compare *plate 15*).

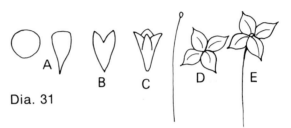

Dia. 31

Maidenhair fern
(*Adiantum raddianum*)

The maidenhair is a graceful and delicate fern, which can be used to great effect in floral arrangements of any kind.

☐ Strip the fronds of a dried maidenhair or asparagus fern (*Asparagus plumosus*) of their foliage.
☐ Roll out green modelling paste thinly, until almost transparent, and cut out a multitude of little leaves (see *diagram 32* for template).
☐ Place the fern skeleton on a board covered with wax paper (do not grease it) and clothe it with leaves. You need only exert slight pressure to make the paste stick to the network of branches.
☐ Leave for several days to dry.
☐ Remove very carefully from the paper, with the aid of a very thin spatula.
☐ Colour the terminal points of the leaves reddish-brown (see *plate 9* on page 19).
☐ Tape the frond to a length of 26 gauge wire if necessary.

Note: The leaves may be frilled before attaching them, but this requires extreme patience as it is a slow, tedious process.

Dia. 32
Maidenhair fern:
template for leaves

Dia. 32

Nasturtium *(Tropaeolum majus)*

The flowers are showy and occur singly in leaf axils. They are made up of five sepals ending in a short or long spur, five irregularly shaped petals, eight stamens and a superior ovary.

Making the stamens
☐ Mould a ball of green paste (about 3 mm in diameter) into a teardrop shape over one end of a length of 26 gauge wire (see *diagram 33A*).
☐ Make three lengthwise incisions in the paste to form a three-lobed ovary (see *diagram 33B*).
☐ Cut eight stamens with very fine anthers to a length of about 20 mm. Arrange these in a circle around the ovary, letting the anthers extend 7 mm beyond it (see *diagram 33C*). Tape them to the wire below the ovary and bend the stem outwards as shown in *diagram 33D*.
☐ Paint the anthers ochre.
☐ *Hint:* If stamens with very small anthers are not available, dip short lengths of thin cotton thread into egg white and then into a mixture of gelatine and colouring powder to form anthers.

Making the sepals and spur
☐ Roll a piece of lemon-coloured paste into a ball about 12 mm in diameter and pinch one end

to form the spur, measuring about 30 mm lengthwise and 4 mm across where it is attached to the ball (see *diagram 33E*).
☐ Flatten the ball slightly, then mould and roll it out into the shape of a Mexican hat. Cut out sepal shapes (see *diagram 34* for template; see also *diagram 33F*).
☐ Thin the edges with a ball tool and cup the sepals slightly. Work the paste with a ball tool so that the spur forms an extension of the upper central sepal. There is a sepal to the left and the right of the latter and two opposite it.
☐ Insert a toothpick or similar instrument into the spur from the end of the upper central sepal and roll it backwards and forwards to hollow it out. Curve the spur slightly outwards.
☐ Pierce the heart of the sepals with the wire to which the stamens are attached to form a hole in the space between the base of the spur and the base of the two lower sepals (see *diagram 33G*). This ensures that, when the sepals have dried and the flower been assembled, the hole will be big enough for the wire (i.e. the stem) to go through.
☐ Using vegetable colouring, paint maroon lines down the centre of the three upper sepals, from the tips right down into the hollowed-out spur. Add one or more lines on either side (see *plate 16* and *diagram 33H*).
☐ Cut out a hole in the centre of a flat piece of foam rubber. Rest the sepals on it, with the spur jutting out at the bottom. Place over a small jar or other hollow container to ensure that the sepals and spur will dry undamaged.

Making the petals
☐ Roll out pale yellow paste very thinly and cut out three irregularly shaped petals (see *diagram 36* for template; see also *diagram 33I*).
☐ Thin the edges with a ball tool and draw fan-like lines from base to edge over the face of each petal (see *diagram 33J*).
☐ Mould the short length of paste at the base of each petal into a roll to form a cauda or tail. Using a veining tool, cut the wings on either side of it at the base to form the beard of the petal (see *diagram 33K*). Bend them upwards.
☐ Attach the petals to the sepals with egg white, covering the spaces as follows: lower left, lower right and finally lower centre, the last petal overlapping the other two on the inside (see *diagram 33L*).
☐ Cut out two more petals, but use a different template (see *diagram 35*). Thin and frill the edges slightly with a ball tool. Vein them like the first three. Cup the lower half of each petal, face side up.

Dia. 33

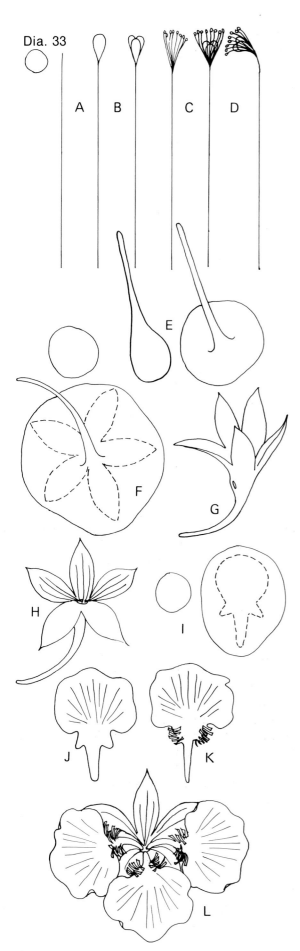

Plate 16
An arrangement of nasturtiums

Dia. 33
Nasturtium: making a flower

Dia. 34
Nasturtium: template for sepals

Dia. 35
Nasturtium: template for large petals

Dia. 36
Nasturtium: template for smaller petals

Dia. 34

Dia. 35

Dia. 36

☐ Form a cup with your thumb, index and middle finger and drape one of the petals over your fingertips, the bulge on the back of the petal resting in the hollow. Curl the edge gently backwards. Repeat with the second petal.

☐ Attach to the sepals with egg white, filling the upper left and then the upper right space.

☐ Allow to dry thoroughly.

☐ Paint the petals with vegetable colouring according to the markings on a specimen flower of the cultivar you wish to make. Use colouring powder for shading.

☐ Paint green lengthwise veins over the back of the sepals and colour the tips with a darker shade of green. Shade further with a trace of the colouring used for the petals.

31

Completing the flower
☐ Apply egg white to a tiny ball of lemon-coloured paste, about 1 mm in diameter, and place it over the hole made in the sepals.
☐ Press the stem, with stamens, through it until the ovary just rests on the ball of paste. Allow to dry.

Making the leaves
☐ Roll out two shades of green paste very thinly and cut out leaves (see *diagram 37* for template). Place a pale green leaf in the cup of a polyurethane apple tray.
☐ Fold a length of wire into a "T" as described on page 23 (see also *diagram 18* on page 24). Apply egg white to the crossbar and push the vertical wire through the paste and polyurethane where the veins of the leaf branch out.

Dia. 37
Nasturtium: template for stem leaves (make larger and smaller versions)

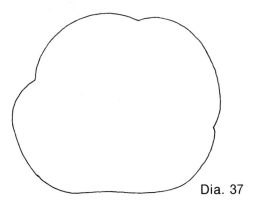

Dia. 37

☐ Cut off the stem of a real leaf, flush with the leaf. Place the leaf over the dark green paste leaf and press down to make veins. Arrange it over the leaf in the polyurethane cup and secure together. Curve the edges of the leaf slightly to make it life-like. Allow to dry.
☐ Accentuate the veins with a lighter shade than that used for the face of the leaf. Colour the edge faintly with red.
☐ Make as many leaves as you need, of varying sizes. Assemble with flowers as desired (see *plate 16* on p. 31).

Orange blossom *(Citrus sinensis)*

The flower consists of four or five sepals, four or five petals, an abundance of stamens and a superior ovary.

Making the ovary
☐ Mould a ball of green paste, about 4 mm in diameter, around a length of 26 gauge wire, 9 mm from one end. Allow to dry.
☐ Mould a ball of white paste, about 3 mm in diameter, around the 9 mm section of wire to form a pistil with a cross-section of 1 mm (see *diagram 38A*). Flatten the paste on top to measure 3 mm in diameter.

Making the stamens
☐ Roll out a piece of white paste very thinly and cut it into a rectangle, 15 mm by a linear measure equal to the circumference of the ovary. Make comblike incisions to obtain very thin strips (stamens) joined at the base by a band of paste, about 2 mm wide (see *diagram 38B*).
☐ Apply egg white to the 2 mm strip and fold it around the ovary. The pistil should be just higher than the stamens (see *diagram 38C*).
☐ Paint the tips of the stamens yellow-brown and the pistil tip yellow-green.

Making the petals
☐ Roll out white paste very thinly (but not transparently thin) and cut out linked petals (see *diagram 40* for template; see also *diagram 38D*).
☐ Thin the edges of each petal with a ball tool and then roll it from the tip to the centre to cup the upper half slightly.
☐ Draw lengthwise veins with a veining tool or a pin on the face of each petal (see *diagram 38E*).
☐ Apply egg white to the base of the petals on the inside and push the stem, with stamens and pistil, through the heart. Secure (see *diagram 39A*).
☐ Arrange the petals as desired: closed, half-open or fully open. Allow to dry.
☐ Roll out a piece of green paste and cut out a calyx shape (see *diagram 41* for template; see also *diagram 39B*). Attach to the base of the dried flower with egg white (see *diagram 39C*).
☐ Paint the heart of the flower and the tips of the petals yellow-green.

Making the buds
☐ For the smallest bud, cut out a calyx as described above and secure a ball of white paste in it with egg white.
☐ For the largest bud, mould a ball of white paste (same size as for the small bud) into an egg shape. Attach to a calyx with egg white.
☐ For the intermediate stages, mould white paste into shapes varying between round and egg-shaped, and attach to calyxes.

Making the leaves
☐ Roll out a piece each of dark green and yellow-green modelling paste. Cut out (see *diagram 42* for template).
☐ Place a piece of fuse wire or 32 gauge wire on the yellow-green leaf and arrange the dark green leaf on top. Press together firmly.
☐ Work the edges with a ball tool and draw a

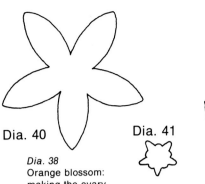

Dia. 42

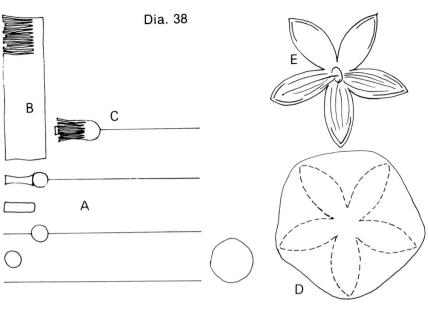

Dia. 38

E

C

B

A

D

Dia. 40   Dia. 41

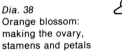

Dia. 38
Orange blossom:
making the ovary,
stamens and petals

Dia. 39
Orange blossom:
assembling the
components

Dia. 40
Orange blossom:
template for petals

Dia. 41
Orange blossom:
template for calyxes

Dia. 42
Orange blossom:
template for stem
leaves (make smaller
and larger versions)

Dia. 39

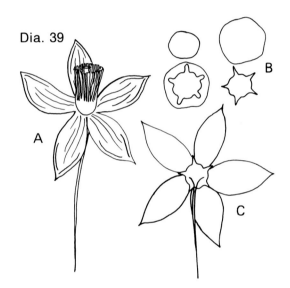

A

B

C

principal vein down the centre from tip to base.
Draw secondary veins branching from it.
☐ Fold the two halves towards each other.
☐ The leaves may vary in size from smaller and
narrower to larger and wider than the template.

Assembling the various parts
☐ Arrange a selection of buds and flowers in a
cluster and tape them to a length of wire.
☐ Add a few leaves opposite each other down
the stem (see *plate 17*).
☐ Note that the blossoms may also be used individually in arrangements.

Plate 17
Individual orange
blossoms and buds
used in an
arrangement

Periwinkles *(Vinca minor)*

The periwinkle is a dwarf sub-shrub with straggling shoots and glossy green or variegated leaves. For cake decorating purposes, the variegated periwinkle can be used most effectively to form lines or fill spaces in an arrangement. The plant bears rosy-purple or white flowers in summer and autumn.

☐ Roll out a piece of white paste very thinly, until almost transparent. Set aside.

☐ Roll out a piece of green paste just as thin and cut out to form an irregularly shaped leaf, slightly smaller than the rolled-out white paste (see *diagram 43* for template). Place on top of the white paste.

☐ Make a second irregularly shaped green leaf. Place it on the other side of the white paste to sandwich the white paste between them.

☐ Roll out the three layers of paste and cut out leaves (see *diagram 44* for template).

Dia. 43
Periwinkle: template for uneven green shape of leaf

Dia. 44
Periwinkle: template for stem leaves (make smaller and larger versions)

Plate 18
An arrangement of tiger lilies and shoots of the variegated periwinkle

Dia. 43

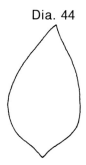

Dia. 44

☐ Cover a piece of fuse wire or 32 gauge wire with green florist's tape and insert it in the base of the leaf. Draw in a central principal vein with secondary veins branching from it.

☐ Make a collection of leaves varying slightly in size and shape, and tape them to a length of 28 gauge wire, arranging them in pairs opposite each other (see *plate 18*). The pairs can be far apart or close together, and you can also use a thinner gauge wire if you wish to make shoots to drape on or hang over a cake.

Tiger lily *(Lilium lancifolium)*

The fiery coloured blooms of this cultivar are regular, their floral parts in units of three. There are six (three plus three) curved, pointed petals with maroon spots, the same ratio of anthers and an ovary made up of six divisions. The ovary is about 15 mm long and is found at the base of an orange-coloured pistil about 45 mm long. If an anther were turned flush against the stamen, the length of these two parts would be equal to that of the pistil plus the ovary, approx. 60 mm.

Making the stamens (six)

☐ Cut a piece of 26 or 28 gauge wire 120 mm long and cover it with white florist's tape. Measure off 70 mm and bend the remaining 50 mm at a right angle (see *diagram 45A*).

☐ Fold the 50 mm section back on itself so that the tip extends 10 mm beyond the angle (see *diagram 45B*). Twist the doubled section tightly to form a "T" (see *diagram 45C*).

☐ Cut off enough wire on either side to obtain a crossbar 8 mm wide (see *diagram 45D*) and turn down the tips slightly.

☐ Colour it orange.

☐ Roll sufficient brown modelling paste into a ball about 3 mm in diameter, flattening it into an oval, and fold it around the crossbar to cover it completely. Cut away the excess paste at the bottom to obtain an anther approximately 2 mm by 10 mm. Hold it between your thumb and index finger, and slit it across the top from end to end (see *diagrams 45E and 45F*). Paint the anther with egg white and dip it in brown colouring powder to give it a velvety finish.

Making the pistil

☐ Cut a piece of 20 gauge wire 150 mm long and roll orange coloured paste around the upper 45 mm (see *diagram 45G*). Mould the paste into a cone 3 mm in diameter at the base and 4 mm in diameter at the top. Cut this cone to obtain a clover shape and pinch the paste to form three little

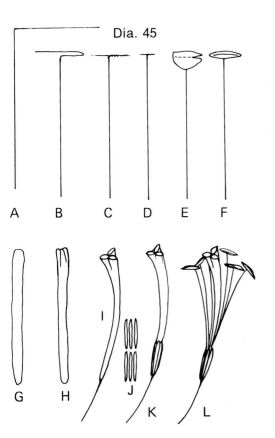

Dia. 45

Flatten the cone on both sides, using a roller and leaving a 30 mm long centre ridge, 3 mm thick at the base and tapering towards the tip.
□ Cut out petals as shown in *diagram 46B* (see *diagrams 47 and 48* on page 36 for templates – make three of each). Thin the edges with a ball tool, taking care not to change the shape of the petal.
□ Hold the petal ridge side up and vein it down the centre. Turn it over and pinch from tip to base to form a rib (see *diagram 46C*).

Dia. 45
Tiger lily: making and assembling the stamens and pistil

Dia. 46
Tiger lily: completing the flower

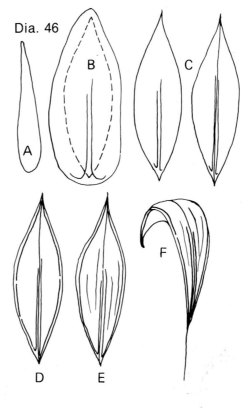

Dia. 46

lobes (see *diagram 45H*). Flatten the pistil across the top and make 5 mm incisions between the lobes (see *diagram 45I*).
□ Paint the tips of the lobes brown, drawing a continuous line about 2 mm long down the centre of each.

Making the ovary
□ Roll six pieces of green paste into little sausage shapes, 15 mm in length and 1 mm in diameter (see *diagram 45J*).
□ Attach them around the base of the pistil, ensuring that the ovary and pistil together are not longer than 60 mm (see *diagram 45K*).

Assembling the stamens and pistil
□ Bend the pistil into a soft curve to give it a natural look.
□ Tape the stamens just below the ovary to the wire protruding from it, placing a stamen in each of the six grooves of the ovary. (The stamens should not be longer than the pistil.) (See *diagram 45L*.)

Making the petals (three plus three)
□ Cut a piece of 26 or 28 gauge wire 40 mm long and cover it with white florist's tape.
□ Roll a piece of orange paste into an upside-down cone 70 mm long, the diameter 10 mm at the base and 5 mm at the top (see *diagram 46A*).

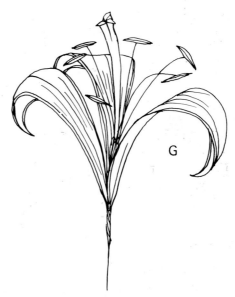

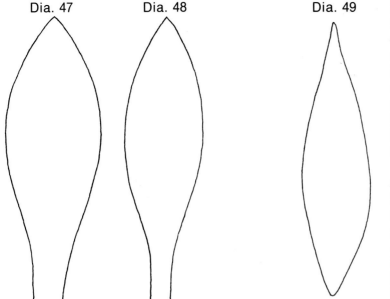

Dia. 47   Dia. 48   Dia. 49

Dia. 47
Tiger lily: template for large petals

Dia. 48
Tiger lily: template for smaller petals

Dia. 49
Tiger lily: template for stem leaves (make smaller and larger versions)

☐ Leave until almost dry.

☐ Dust the lower half of the petal with dark orange powder and paint maroon spots over this section (note that the tiger lily differs from other *Lilium* species in that its petals are not spotted all over). Dust the lower 10 mm at the base with green colouring powder.

☐ Turn the petal over and dust the entire surface with dark orange colouring powder. Colour the tip green.

Assembling the flower

☐ Tape the three larger petals, evenly spaced, around the ovary, with every second stamen opposite the middle of each petal (see *diagram 46G*).

☐ Tape the narrower petals opposite the remaining stamens in the spaces.

☐ Apply egg white to the stem at the base of the flower, mould a small ball of green paste around it and smooth the paste over the petals with a modelling tool. (See *plate 18* on page 34.)

Making the leaves

☐ Roll out green paste and cut it into leaves (see *diagram 49* for template).

☐ Working with a veining tool, make a principal vein down the centre and, as for the petals, draw a few lengthwise secondary veins on either side of it.

☐ Insert green florist's wire at the base, curve the leaf and allow it to dry.

☐ Make as many as required.

☐ Use with flowers in arrangements as desired.

☐ Turn the petal over again and draw a line on either side of the principal vein to form two full-length lip-like structures.

☐ Draw a thin line, about 0,5 mm from the edge, along the outline of the petal (see *diagram 46D*). Roll these strips inwards to form a cupped edge.

☐ Draw a few lengthwise veins on either side of the lip-like structures (see *diagram 46E*).

☐ Insert a piece of 10 mm long wire in the thickened base of the petal and bend it slightly, then bend the tip of the petal backwards to form a question mark (see *diagram 46F*).

Plate 19 (opposite page)
Multi-purpose cake, combining the techniques of flooding and lacework (see *diagram 50* for patterns of the collars and ovals, and pages 10 to 11 and 16 for methods) To indicate the position of the top collar, use a template of the pattern to make markings on the cake. Attach with royal icing. Sprays of flowers (in this case a combination of apple blossoms, roses and lilac) and ovals (placed at an angle) are added consecutively. The collar on the board is finished off with groupings of small flowers and buds

Cakes for various occasions

The ingredients for fruit cakes are expensive and decorating is usually connected with a special occasion such as an engagement, kitchen tea, wedding, christening, wedding anniversary, birthday, confirmation or Christmas. Consequently there is little room for making mistakes. To ensure success, you need to be equipped with good recipes and patterns (see Chapters 1 and 4).

In addition, you should be able to set about your decorating task with confidence (all the cakes in this section can be made on the basis of the guidelines given in Chapters 1 and 2).

The full-colour photographs that follow are grouped according to technique rather than occasion, and are accompanied by detailed captions.

Cakes decorated with filigree, lace and built-up line or extension and bridge work

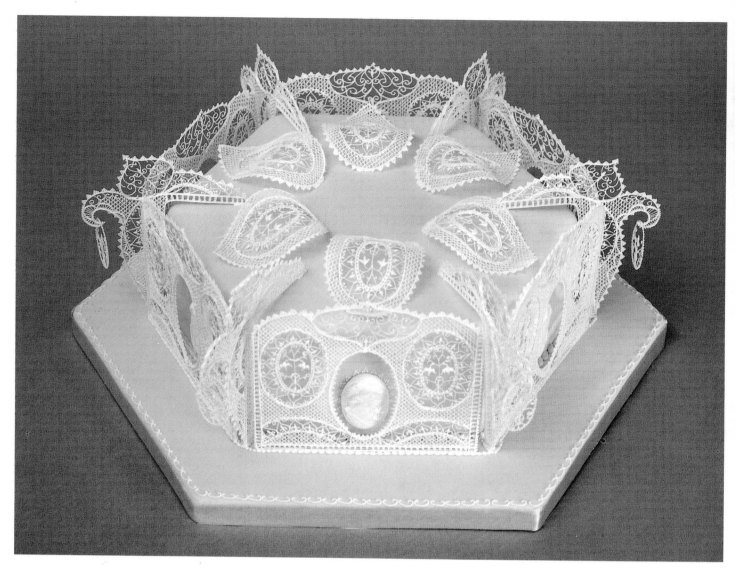

Plate 20

Six-sided wedding cake with cameos (see *diagrams 51 to 54* for filigree patterns). Use a template of the pattern for the side panels and mark off ovals around the side of the cake. Attach either cameos or arrangements of flowers in these spaces. Finish off with piped designs if necessary.

Make markings on the cake for the positioning of the wings with the aid of an appropriate template. Draw a hexagonal line on the board around the cake, 10 mm from its base. Following your markings, pipe royal icing on top of the cake and on the board for attaching one of the wings. Carefully place in position, support it on either side with pieces of sponge and allow to set.

Attach a second wing at the next corner in the same way. When set, pipe a strip of royal icing on the line on the board between the two filigree pieces. Carefully place the base of a prepared side panel on this piping and let it rest against the top edge of the cake.

Place a block of sponge, 60 × 60 × 20 mm, on the cake opposite the middle of the side panel and move it gently forwards until it pushes the filigree piece into a vertical position. Support it with sponge to prevent its falling over. Repeat this procedure right around the cake until all the wings and side panels are in position. Allow to dry thoroughly and remove all the pieces of sponge very carefully.

As can be seen in the photograph, the filigree decorations for the top of the cake are piped on curved shapes. Attach in position with royal icing.

Piping finishes off the bottom edges of both the filigree pieces and the board.

A bride, vase of flowers or other sugar object may be placed in the middle of the cake to mark a particular occasion

38

Plate 21
Two-tiered filigree wedding cake with agapanthus blooms and buds (see *diagrams 55 to 58* for patterns and pages 17 to 18 for instructions for making the flowers).

The two cakes, including the marzipan and plastic icing covering, measure 165 × 165 mm and 260 × 260 mm respectively.

For best results, it is best to draw your patterns and pipe them once the cakes have been prepared, as slight adjustments to the patterns in the book may be necessary. Work from top to bottom.

Mark the correct positions for the centre pieces on top of the smaller cake by means of a pricked-out cross stretching from side to side and not from corner to corner. Pipe a line in royal icing from the centre outwards to attach one piece. Handle it with a paintbrush as described on page 11 and support it with pieces of sponge to prevent it toppling over, and ensuring that it stands in a vertical position. Allow to set. Add a second piece in the same way opposite, not next to, the first one, piping royal icing down the inner edge of the latter so that they are joined together in the centre. When dry, add the remaining pieces in similar stages.

Make floral arrangements on small pieces of plastic icing to fill the spaces between the filigree uprights and attach with royal icing. (Note: Because filigree work is so fragile, it would be unwise to make your arrangements directly on the cake.)

Draw a line on the bottom cake right around the bottom edge of the top cake, about 45 mm from its base, and mark the centre of all the sides both on the lines just drawn and on the top edges of the small cake. Pipe a strip of royal icing (the length of one side panel) along the middle of one of the four drawn lines. Attach and centre a prepared filigree panel, letting it rest against the top edge of the top tier. Repeat right around the cake.

Place small arrangements of flowers on the corners *within* the boundaries of the drawn lines. Attach the corner panels to cover the floral arrangements (I chose to make eight halves rather than four right-angled pieces – see caption for *diagram 55*).

Pipe a line of small dots down all the joins and along the bottom edges of the panels, or decorate this edging with a snail's trail. Attach lace pieces to the top edges of the panels, letting them lean slightly towards you (it would be best to handle them with a paintbrush, particularly near the top decoration).

Move to the bottom tier.

Draw a line on the board right around the large cake, about 45 mm from its base, and mark the centre of all the sides both on the lines just drawn and on the top edge of the cake. First attach one centre panel as described above, then another so that the two meet exactly in the middle and lean against the top edge of the cake. Repeat this procedure right around; then place your floral arrangements at the corners within the border lines. Cover the corners and do the finishing off as for the top tier

Plate 22

Filigree wedding cake with bride and arch (see *diagrams 59 to 67* for patterns).

Prepare the cake (it should be 20 cm in diameter), six-sided board, bride, platform (it is made from pastillage and consists of three steps each about 3 mm high), filigree pieces and collar.

Use a template of the collar pattern to make markings on the cake for its positioning. Pipe stars about 5 mm high accordingly and attach the collar.

Place the platform in the middle of the cake and position the bride on it.

Assemble the vault and side panels of the arch, and once set lift over the bride with a paintbrush. Attach to the cake with royal icing. (Note: The side panels of the arch have to be exactly vertical, otherwise stress from the vault will cause

them to bend and snap.) Place floral arrangements in the inner scallops of the collar and then move on to the lower section of the cake.

Place six arrangements of flowers on the board opposite the sides, not the corners, of the hexagon. Make markings between them to correspond exactly to the corners of the collar on top of the cake. Pipe dots in royal icing from one corner halfway to the next along the edge of the collar; also pipe a 20 mm row of dots in the same direction on the board from the corner of the corresponding marking. Attach a prepared filigree panel. Attach a mirror image of this panel in the same way to form an archway. Repeat right around the cake.

Pipe dots down all the joins of the panels and attach pendant lace pieces to the centre of the vaults of the bottom arches. The board is finished off with scalloped piping

Plate 23
Close-up of bride on filigree wedding cake with arches

Plate 24
Close-up of a bottom arch of the filigree wedding cake with
bride and arches

Plate 25

Wedding cake with orange blossoms, combining the techniques of filigree and built-up line work (see *diagrams 68 to 73* for patterns and pages 32 to 33 for instructions for making the flowers).

Use a template of *diagram 68* to make markings on the cake for the positioning of the centre pieces (see dotted lines radiating from the centre). Also mark the correct positions of the five wings and the built-up line work between them. Prick out the lines of the bottom design.

The built-up line work over the edge of the cake is done first: Following *diagram 72* and using royal icing and a No. 0 tube, pipe straight lines 2 to 3 mm apart, from the centre to the left and then from the centre to the right of the design (or the other way round). Move five lines to the left and pipe a diagonal line from the top of the design to the central point at the bottom. Using this as your guide, pipe diagonal lines (also 2 to 3 mm apart) to the left and the right over the first set of straight lines.

Reverse the second procedure to obtain diagonal lines that slant from top right to bottom left.

Change to a No. 00 tube and repeat the three stages of piping to obtain a built-up design consisting of six layers of lines. (If you wish to create a dome shape, follow the instructions set out on page 12.)

To finish off the piping on the side of the cake, first make dots with a No. 0 tube and then squiggles about 2 mm wide with a No. 00 tube (see pattern).

Once the top designs have been completed, repeat the piping procedure, following the pricked-out lines of the bottom design.

Assemble floral arrangements on the cake as shown in the photograph, and attach the pieces of the centre decoration according to the description given for that of the two-tiered filigree wedding cake (see caption of *plate 21*).

Attach the wings as described for the six-sided wedding cake with cameos (see caption of *plate 20*).

Add the floral arrangements on the board

Plate 26
Small wedding cake
with roses, carnations,
lilacs and baby's
breath, finished off
with built-up line work
(see pages 12, 22 and
29, as well as
diagrams 74 to 76)

Plate 27
Multi-purpose cake
with built-up line work
made by Cynthia
Fletcher (see page 12
for method and
diagrams 77 to 79 for
patterns)

Plate 28
One-tiered wedding cake with carnations and broom (see pages 22 to 23) made by Cynthia Fletcher. The bottom edge of the cake is finished off with extension and bridge work (see pages 13 to 14) and the board with built-up line work (see page 12)

Plate 29
Three-tiered wedding cake with broom, flame lilies and honeysuckle (see pages 22 to 29), finished off with extension and bridge work (see pages 13 to 14)

44

Plate 30
The bottom tier of the
cake in *plate 29* can be
used as a single
wedding cake

Cakes with pastillage decorations

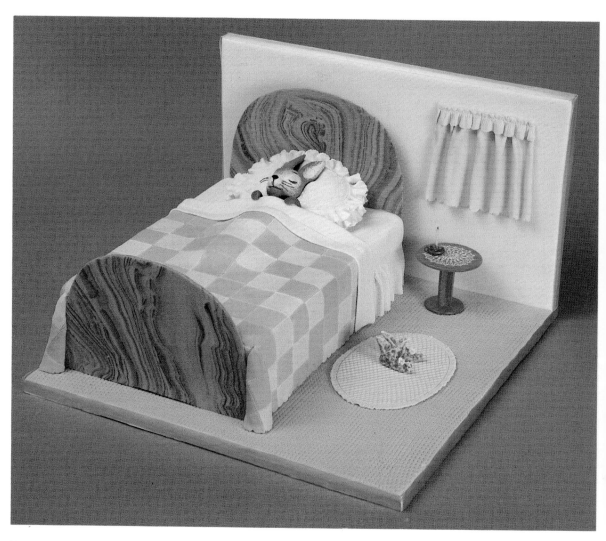

Plate 31

Child's birthday cake with bunny (see *diagram 84* for pattern of head-board and foot of bed).

The board for the floor is square and that for the wall is as wide but only three-quarters as high. Cover the wall with plastic icing in a colour of your choice. Make a curtain from plastic icing and attach in position; allow to dry. Cover the floor with plastic icing and form a design over it with a rolling-pin. Join the two parts at right angles. Place a baked 200 × 300 × 70 mm cake in position to form the bed.

The head-board and foot is made from pastillage, the night frill from modelling paste and the bottom sheet from plastic icing (attach in this order). Add an indented plastic icing pillow with two modelling paste frills and embroider the slip as desired.

Mould modelling paste in a cast to form the bunny's head and neck (you can make your own cast by using quick-drying putty or plaster of Paris and a plastic toy bunny of a suitable

size). Paint and add whiskers as shown in the photograph. Place in position on the pillow and add a sausage shape for the body.

Drape a piece of rolled-out white plastic icing over the bunny as if covering it with a sheet.

The patchwork blanket is made from plastic icing to which gum tragacanth or CMC is added (about 2 ml to a ball about 50 mm in diameter). The squares measure about 30 × 30 mm and can be made in colours of your own choice. They are placed in position block by block, and special care should be taken with the draped corners at the foot of the bed.

Roll out a piece of white plastic icing and cut a strip about 50 mm wide and long enough to reach over the bed, matching up with the blanket on either side. Fold in a 20 mm wide strip lengthwise. Make a line of stitching on the opposite side, about 10 mm from the edge. Place over the bed with the folded end towards the bunny's head. Make two

46

front legs with paws and push them under the blanket so that just the paws show.

Place a rug in front of the bed (made according to your choice) and put a pair of "magic shoes" on top of it. They are made by rolling a piece of modelling paste into a cone about 30 mm long and 5 mm across at the wide end. Bend this end upwards and hollow it out with a skewer (the shoe should now measure about 20 mm from toe to heel). Curl the tip back and paint with multi-coloured flecks. Attach a flower to the bridge of the shoe.

The bedside table is made from pastillage, the top measuring 65 mm and the base 40 mm in diameter. Pipe a doily on the table top and place a candlestick (pastillage, shaped in a shallow hollow container about 15 mm in diameter) with candle (made from modelling paste) on it

Plate 32

Birthday cake for a handyman (see *diagram 85* for patterns of the hammer and saw). Cover the cake and board with grained plastic icing, and make the hammer and saw from pastillage. To form shavings, roll out modelling paste very thinly and cut into equal width strips with a parsley cutter. Wind them around a wooden skewer to form coils; allow to set slightly, then remove to dry completely. Make the nails from modelling paste, using a real nail as model. Assemble on the cake as shown in the photograph, and trim with flowers and a cord made from plastic icing with a clay gun, using a round disc about 1 mm in diameter

Cakes with flooded decorations

Plate 33
Christening cake (see *diagram 86* for pattern). Flood the pillow, baby, blanket and top collar. Also flood the collar on the board. Use a template of the pattern for the top collar and make markings for its correct position. Attach with royal icing. Trim with flowers and add the baby's name

Plate 35 (opposite page)
Birthday cake for a little boy (see diagrams *88 to 91* for patterns). Flood the boys, as well as the tennis rackets, cricket bats and balls (the strings of the rackets were piped with royal icing and a No. 00 tube). After covering the cake, draw lines in the paste (I coloured mine antique white) with a veining tool to mark off four sections, and pipe brown royal icing into these grooves. Paint the backgrounds with vegetable colouring and pipe royal icing flowers on the cake. Place the figures and items in position and attach with royal icing

Plate 34
Christening cake (see *diagram 87* for pattern). Flood the top collar as well as the one on the board. Trim the cake around the base with arrangements of daisies and add the baby's name, or place a filigree or pastillage cradle in the centre

Plate 36
Birthday cake for the more mature man (see *diagram 92* for pattern). Flood the collar and also flood separate leaves and bunches of grapes for the board. Add the name, and finish off the cake with tendrils (use royal icing and a No. 0 tube) and curved lacework (see *diagram 102* for a selection of patterns)

Plate 37
Engagement cake (see *diagram 93* for pattern). Flood the figures, paint the background with vegetable colouring and pipe royal icing flowers directly onto the cake. Attach the boy and girl, then finish off the top edge with lacework (see *diagram 102* for a selection of patterns). Pipe an embroidery design around the sides of the cake (see *diagrams 103 to 119* for a selection of patterns) and repeat the design on the board. Trim with floral arrangements in the corners (I used roses, carnations and marguerites)

Plate 38
Close-up of engagement cake

Plate 39
Confirmation cake (see *diagram 94* for pattern). Flood the girl
from her waist upwards (the skirt is made from modelling
paste), and also flood the window and candle. Add the skirt
after the flooded pieces have been attached in position (the
skirt is made from a crescent shape, cut from a semicircle,
to fit it around the waist). The bird is formed by figure piping
and the flowers (roses and five-petalled blossoms), ribbon
and bow are made from modelling paste. The side of the
cake is decorated with garlands of royal icing blossoms and
forget-me-nots, trimmed with flooded bows

Plate 40
Christmas cake made by Cynthia Fletcher (see *diagram 95* for pattern). The harp, holly, figures and sheet music are flooded or piped separately and attached to the cake when dry. The border design is, however, pricked out and flooded directly onto the cake

Plate 41
Close-up of the built-up line work around the base of the Christmas cake with harpist (prick out the pattern on the cake and use a succession of tubes No. 2, 1, 0 and 00 for the piping – see page 12 for details of this decorating technique)

Plate 42
Christmas cake featuring the three wise men, made by
Cynthia Fletcher (see *diagrams 96 to 98* for patterns). Flood
the figures separately and attach to the cake with royal icing.
Note that, for perspective, the front figure on the right is
raised about 5 mm by placing a roll of paste underneath it
(plastic icing rocks prevent it from seeming to float in the air)

Miscellaneous cakes

Plate 43
Cake for a kitchen tea, or a woman who loves pottering about in the kitchen (see pages 30 to 32 for detailed instructions for making nasturtiums). The strainer (shaped over a real one and the mesh piped with royal icing and a No. 00 tube), as well as the teacloth were made from modelling paste. Paint the stripes and drape the cloth while the paste is still pliable. The teapot is a round cake covered with plastic icing. The spout, handle and lid are also plastic icing, but the mixture was strengthened by the addition of a little gum tragacanth

Plate 44
Close-up of the edging around the base of the cake with nasturtiums. The piping was done in royal icing with a No. 42 Bekenal tube and a No. 0 writing tube

Plate 45
Birthday cake for a one-year-old child, made by Frances Bell
(see *diagram 99* for pattern). Use a No. 00 tube and royal
icing for all the decorating. Proceed as follows: Pipe design
of bear on a piece of ungreased glass and allow it to dry.
Cover cake and make a bear impression in the paste with
the piped design before it has set – this is preferable to the
pin-prick method). Decorate with piped dots and lines. The
daisies around the edge of the cake and board were
prepared beforehand but their leaves and stems, as well as
the forget-me-nots, were piped directly onto the covering.
The scalloped edgings were formed by overpiping in two
colours, using tubes No. 1 and 0. An easy and effective cake
for the beginner

Plate 46
Birthday cake with Peruvian lilies (see pages 18 to 20 for
detailed instructions for making these flowers)

Plate 47
Cake for an engagement or St. Valentine's day (see *diagram 100* for pattern). Cut out hearts from plastic icing according to the diagram and set aside to dry. Flood the cherubs and allow to set. Make a ruffle from plastic icing to which gum tragacanth has been added for strength. Cut out miniature hearts (keep to decorate the board and sides of the cake) and attach the ruffle to the outer edge of the covered cake. Place the prepared hearts on top of the cake to cover the inner edge of the ruffle, position the cherubs and trim with paste ribbons and flowers. Finish off the board and sides of the cake with the miniature hearts cut from the ruffle

Plate 48

Cake for a 50th wedding anniversary (see pages 26 to 27 for
detailed instructions for making fuchsias). Bake two
rectangular cakes 150 × 230 × 20 mm. Cover with
marzipan, then cover two short and one long side with white
plastic icing; make impressions with a sterilised ruler to form
pages.
Roll out coloured plastic icing for one of the covers and
proceed as follows: Cut the cover according to the length
and twice the width, plus 30 mm, of the pages; place on a
sheet of plastic, then put the cake on top of it, to one side, so
that the pages face outwards. Fold the rest of the icing over
the cake with the aid of the plastic sheet, forming a rounded
back for the book. Decorate with gilt embroidery which
stretches over the back as well, and add the wording. Make
a second book, but omit the ''title''.
Assemble on a board as in photograph and decorate with
sprays of flowers. The embroidery finishing on the board was
done with royal icing and a No. 0 Bekenal tube (see *diagrams
103 to 119* for a selection of patterns)

Plate 49
Christmas, wedding or anniversary cake (see *diagram 101* for pattern of bells). Make bells from pastillage shaped over a curved object and use plastic icing for the clappers. Assemble on top of the cake with a spray of small orchids, lilac, carnations, blossoms and maidenhair fern. Embroidery done in royal icing with a No. 0 tube finishes off the sides of the cake (see *diagrams 103 to 119* for a selection of patterns)

Plate 50
Close-up of embroidery design and piping on board of multi-purpose cake depicted in *plate 49*

Patterns

**Patterns for cakes decorated
with filigree, lace and built-up
line work
(designed by Margie Smuts)**

Dia. 50

Dia. 50
Multi-purpose cake
(see *plate 19*): pattern
for collar and
overlapping ovals

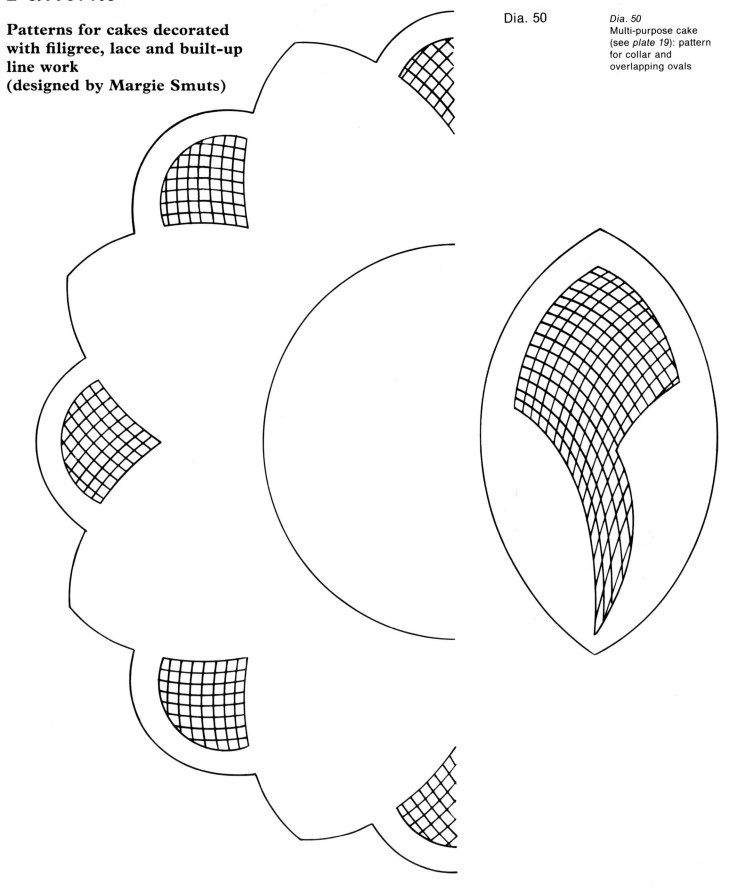

Dia. 51

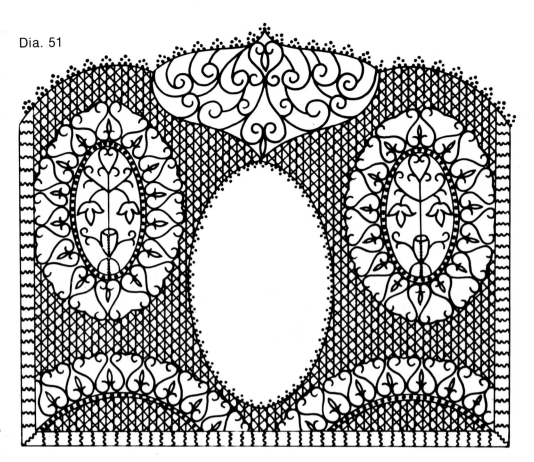

Dia. 51
Side panel for six-sided wedding cake with cameos (see *plate 20*)

Dia. 52
Cameo wedding cake: medallion for hanging on hook of wing

Dia. 53
Wing of cameo wedding cake

Dia. 53

Dia. 52

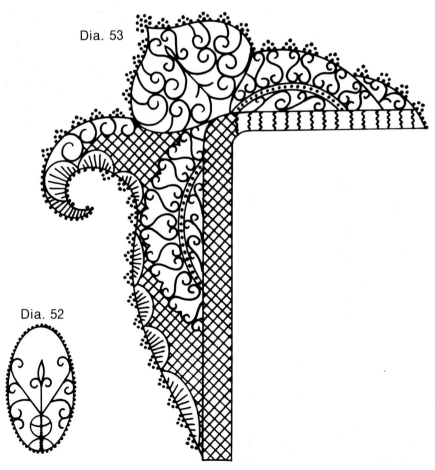

Dia. 54

Dia. 55

Dia. 56

Dia. 54
Pattern for decorations on top of cameo wedding cake (note: they must be piped over a curved object, as can be seen in *plate 20*)

Dia. 55
Corner panel for two-tiered filigree wedding cake with agapanthus blooms and buds (see *plate 21*). This design must be piped over an object bent at right angles. You may, however, make it in two halves, omitting the top and bottom centre motifs and using grid piping instead (I chose to do this)

Dia. 56
Side panel for two-tiered filigree wedding cake

Dia. 57

Dia. 58

Dia. 57
Lace decoration for top
edge of side panels of
two-tiered filigree
wedding cake

Dia. 58
Centre piece for top
decoration of two-
tiered filigree wedding
cake

Dia. 59
Vault for arch of
filigree wedding cake
with bride, to be piped
over an object bent at
right angles (see
plates 22 and 23)

Dia. 59   A

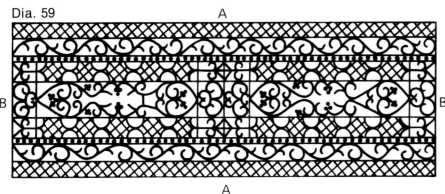

B   B

A

Dia. 60   B

Dia. 60
Side panel for arch of
filigree wedding cake
with bride

Dia. 61

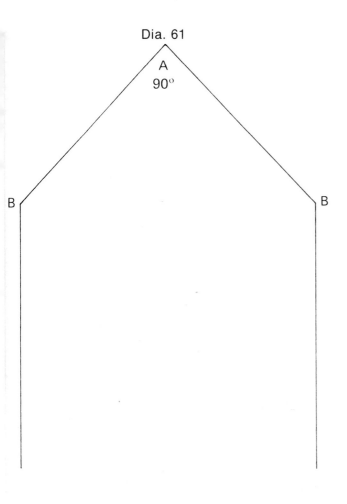

A
90°

B   B

Dia. 61
Front view of arch over bride

Dia. 62
Trellis pattern for vault of filigree wedding cake with bride (note: the end piece on the far right is positioned in the top 90° corner of *diagram 61*)

Dia. 63
Side panel for bottom arches of filigree wedding cake with bride (note: a mirror image of this pattern completes the arch)

Dia. 64
Lace decoration suspended from centre join of bottom arch of filigree wedding cake with bride

Dia. 62

Dia. 63

Dia. 64

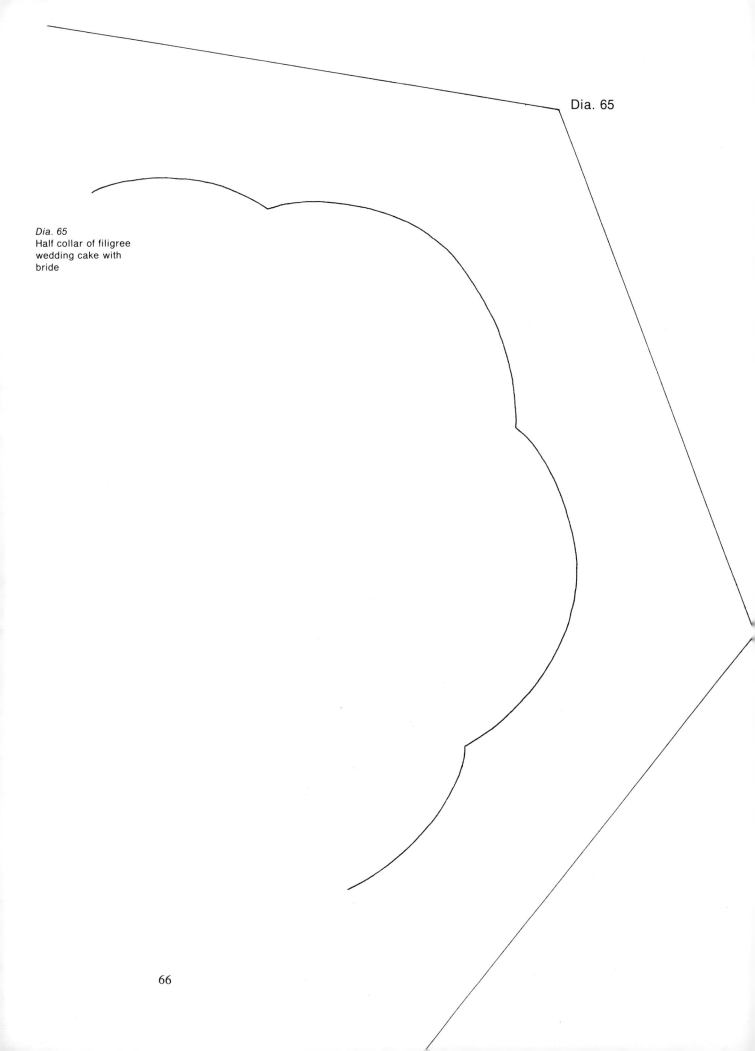

Dia. 65

Dia. 65
Half collar of filigree
wedding cake with
bride

Dia. 66

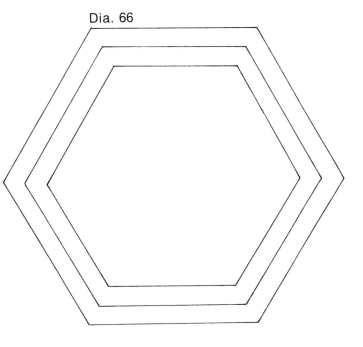

Dia. 67

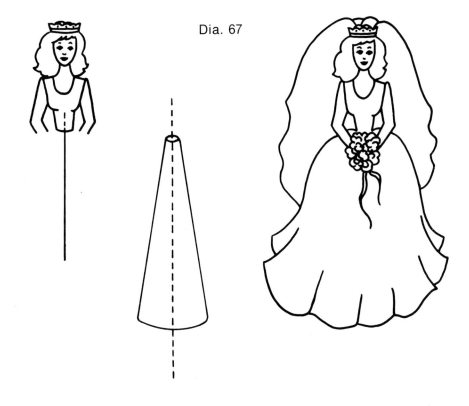

Dia. 66
Platform for bride of
filigree wedding cake
with arch

Dia. 67
Pattern of bride for
filigree wedding cake
with arch

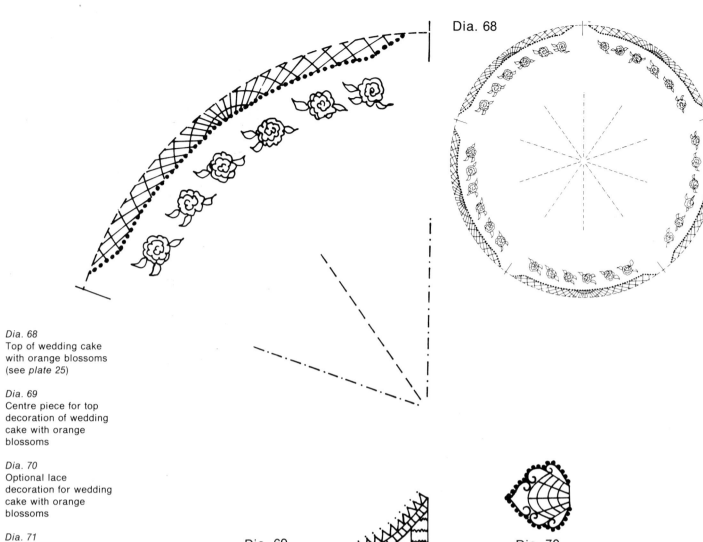

Dia. 68

Dia. 68
Top of wedding cake
with orange blossoms
(see *plate 25*)

Dia. 69
Centre piece for top
decoration of wedding
cake with orange
blossoms

Dia. 70
Optional lace
decoration for wedding
cake with orange
blossoms

Dia. 71
Wing of wedding cake
with orange blossoms

Dia. 69

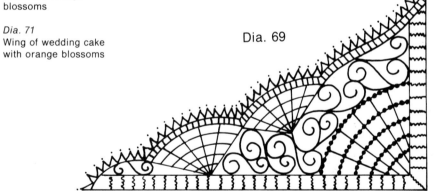

Dia. 70

Dia. 71

Dia. 72

Dia. 72
Pattern for built-up line
work on wedding cake
with orange blossoms

Dia. 73
Pattern for built-up line
work on board of cake
with orange blossoms

Dia. 73

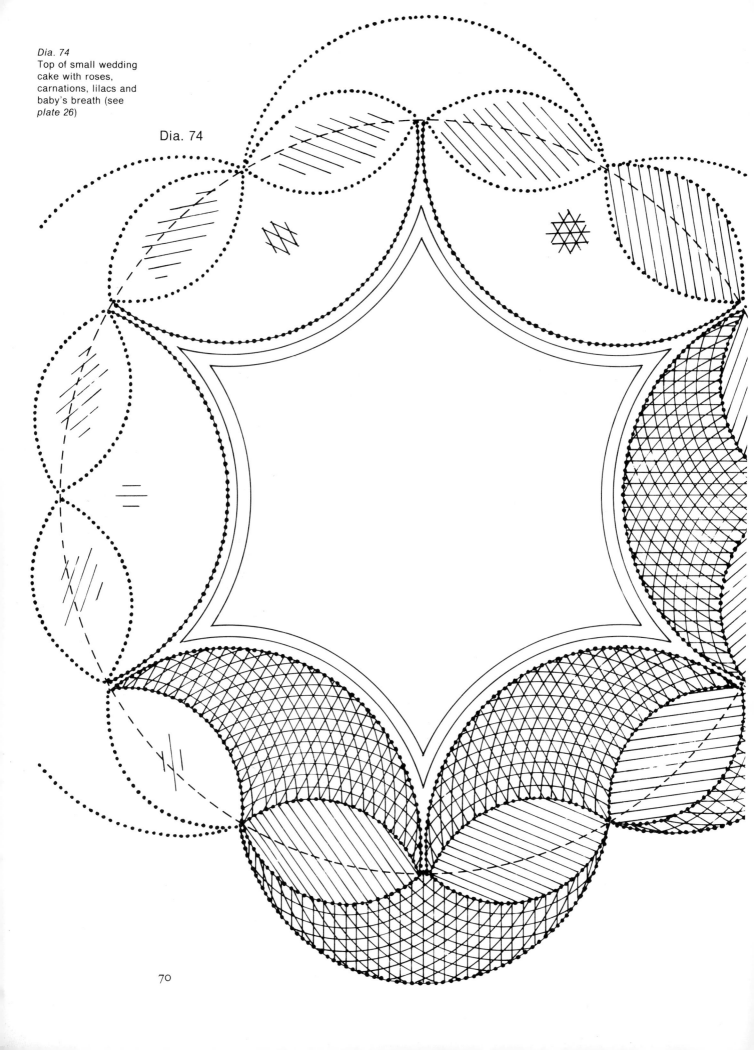

Dia. 74
Top of small wedding
cake with roses,
carnations, lilacs and
baby's breath (see
plate 26)

Dia. 74

70

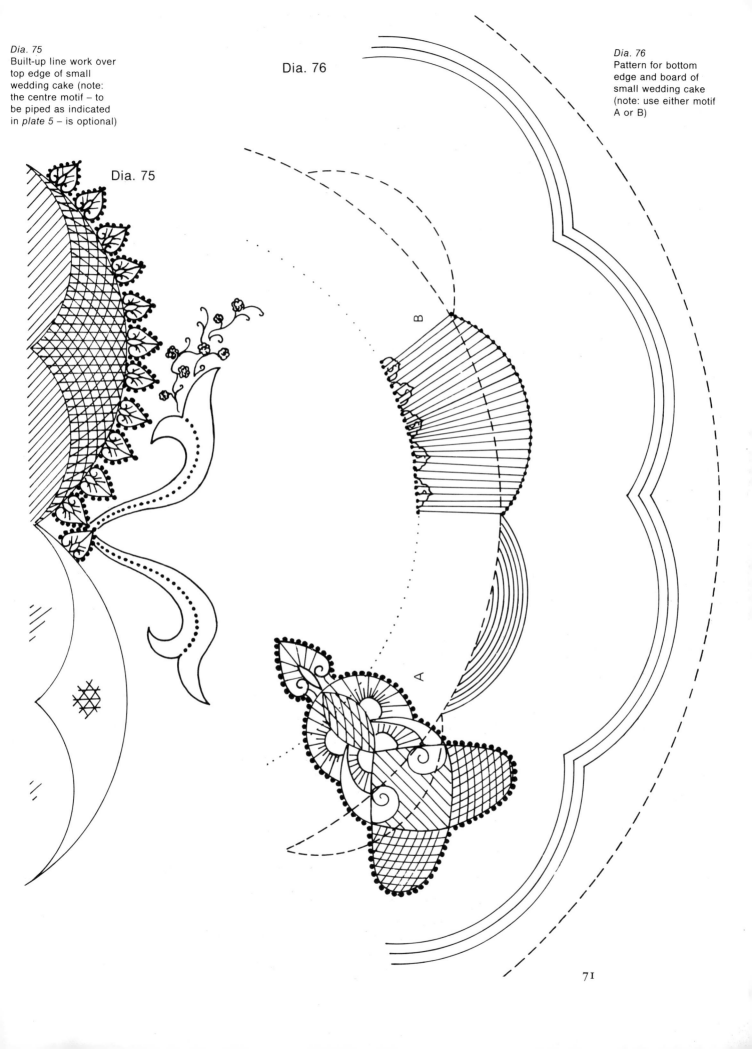

Dia. 75
Built-up line work over
top edge of small
wedding cake (note:
the centre motif – to
be piped as indicated
in *plate 5* – is optional)

Dia. 76

Dia. 75

Dia. 76
Pattern for bottom
edge and board of
small wedding cake
(note: use either motif
A or B)

B

A

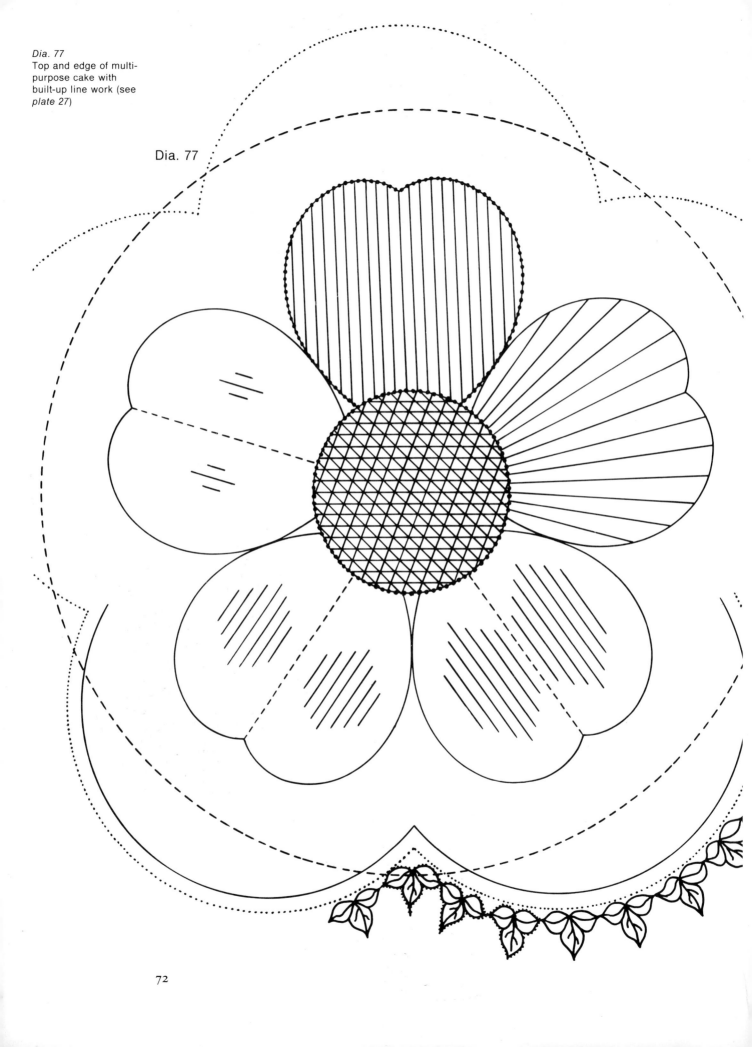

Dia. 77
Top and edge of multi-
purpose cake with
built-up line work (see
plate 27)

Dia. 77

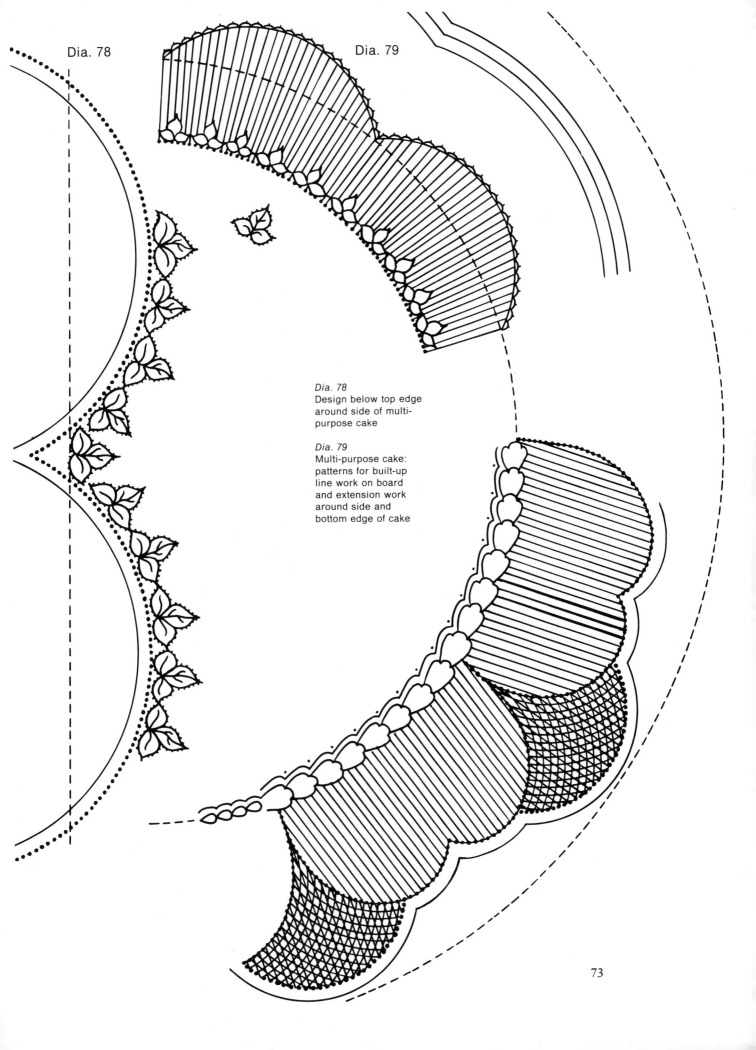

Dia. 78

Dia. 79

Dia. 78
Design below top edge
around side of multi-
purpose cake

Dia. 79
Multi-purpose cake:
patterns for built-up
line work on board
and extension work
around side and
bottom edge of cake

73

Patterns for cakes with pastillage decorations

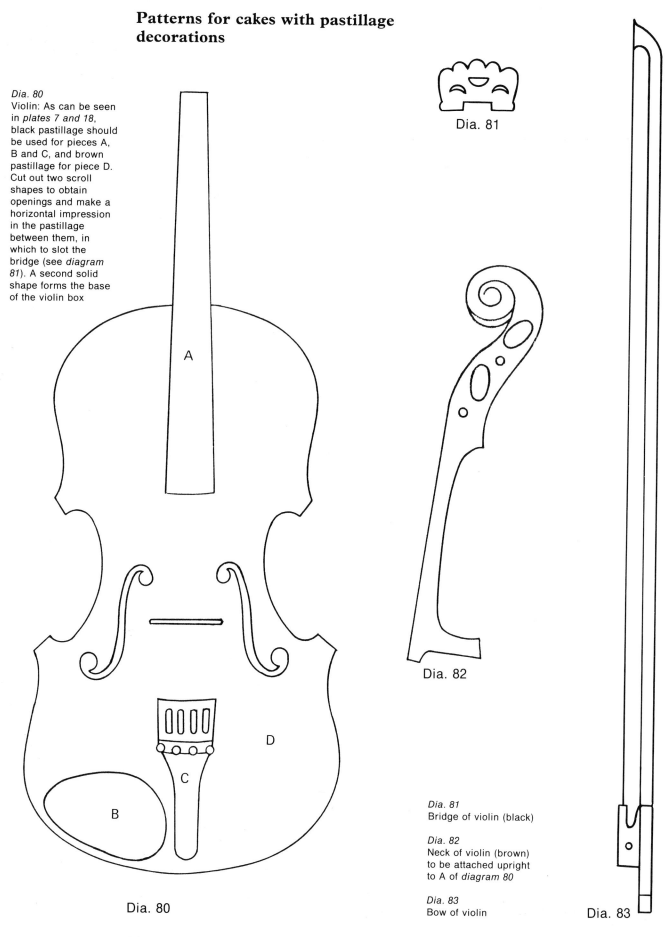

Dia. 80
Violin: As can be seen in *plates 7 and 18*, black pastillage should be used for pieces A, B and C, and brown pastillage for piece D. Cut out two scroll shapes to obtain openings and make a horizontal impression in the pastillage between them, in which to slot the bridge (see *diagram 81*). A second solid shape forms the base of the violin box

Dia. 81

Dia. 82

Dia. 80

Dia. 81
Bridge of violin (black)

Dia. 82
Neck of violin (brown) to be attached upright to A of *diagram 80*

Dia. 83
Bow of violin

Dia. 83

Dia. 84
Head-board (outer
line) and foot (inner
line) for child's
birthday cake with
bunny (see *plate 31*)

Dia. 84

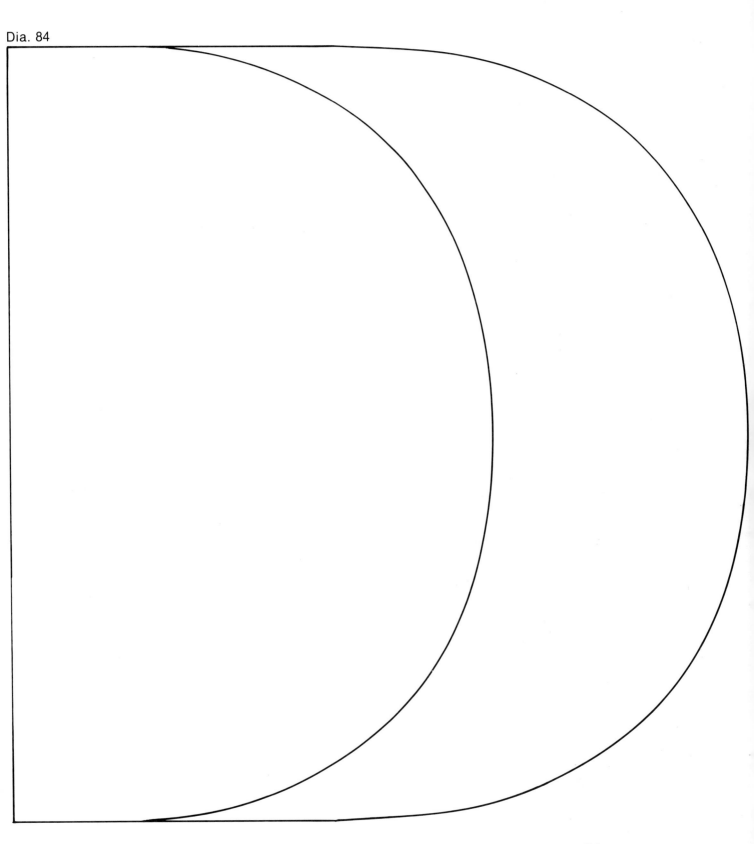

Dia. 85
Hammer and saw for a
handyman's birthday
cake (see *plate 32*).
The handle (brown)
and blade (grey) of the
saw are made
separately

Dia. 85

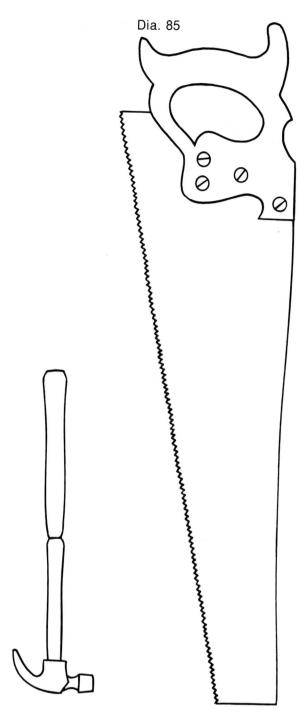

Patterns for cakes with flooded decorations

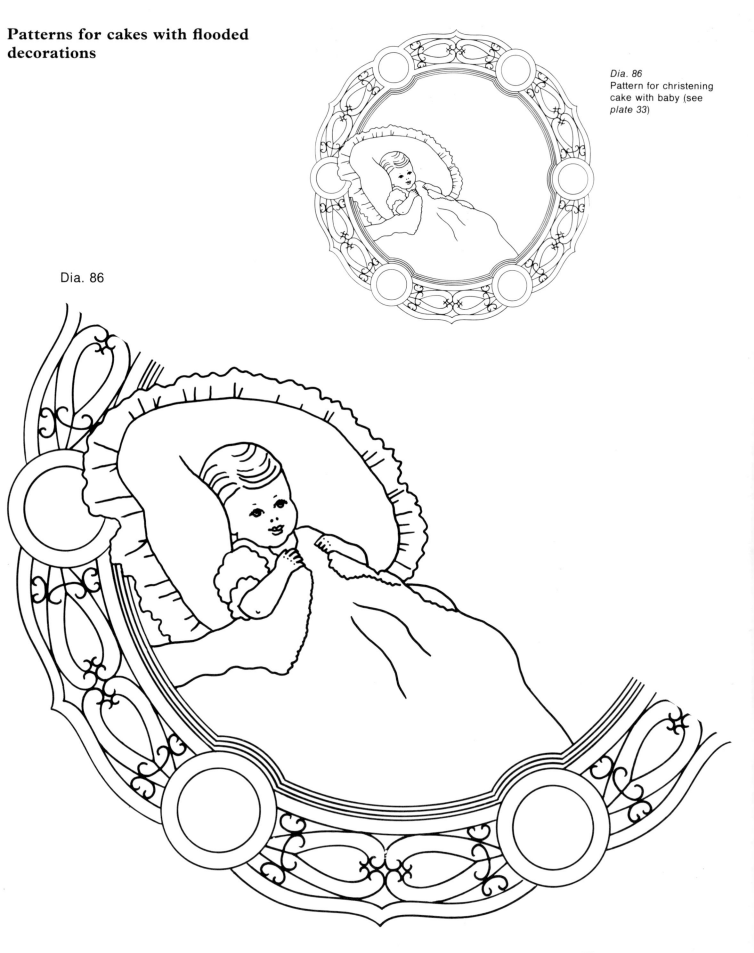

Dia. 86

Dia. 86
Pattern for christening cake with baby (see *plate 33*)

Dia. 87
Pattern for christening
cake with storks (see
plate 34). Note: the
stork motifs may be
replaced by the motif
with doves for an
Easter cake

Dia. 88

Dia. 89

Dia. 90
Cricket player

Dia. 91
Soccer player (note:
the four young
sportsmen may either
be used individually or
grouped together, as
in *plate 35*, for a little
boy's birthday)

Dia. 90

Dia. 91

Dia. 92

Dia. 92
Pattern with grapes
and vine leaves (see
plate 36, birthday cake
for the more mature
man)

Dia. 93
Pattern for an
engagement cake (see
plates 37 and 38)

Dia. 93

Dia. 94

Dia. 94
Pattern for a
confirmation cake (see
plate 39)

Dia. 95
Pattern for a Christmas
cake (see *plate 40*)

Dia. 95

Silent
Night

Dia. 96

Dia. 97

Dia. 98
Wise man with gold
(see *plate 42* for a
grouping of the three
figures)

Dia. 98

Patterns for miscellaneous cakes

Dia. 99
Pattern of bear for a
one-year-old's birthday
(see *plate 45*)

Dia. 99

Dia. 100

Dia. 100
Pattern for an
engagement or St.
Valentine's day cake
(see *plate 47*)

Dia. 101
Pattern of bell for
multi-purpose cake
(see *plate 49*)

Dia. 101

Dia. 102

Dia. 102
*Progressives of ten
lacework patterns*

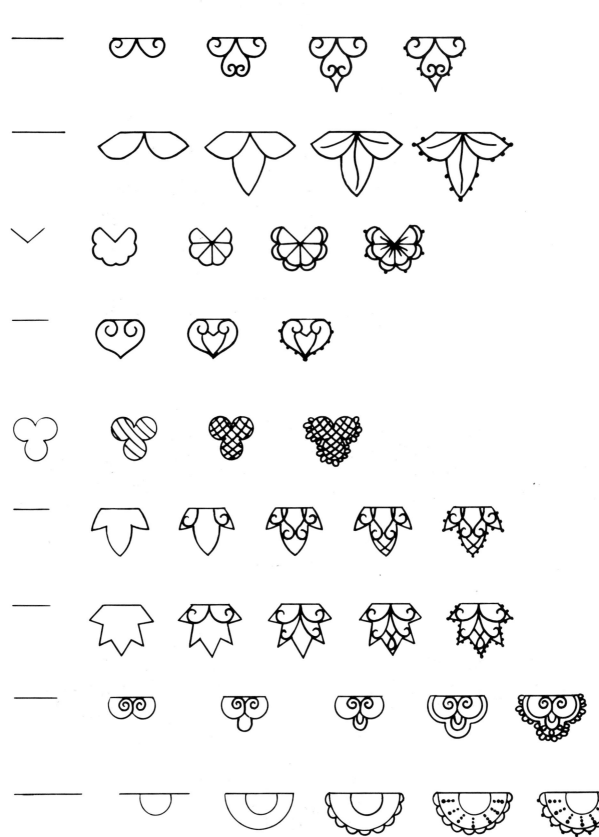

Embroidery patterns

Dia. 103

Dia. 104

Dia. 105

Dia. 106

Dia. 107

Dia. 108

Dia. 109

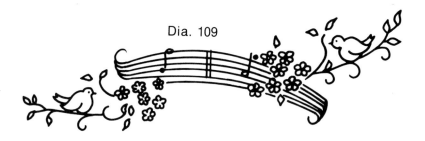

Dia. 110

Dia. 111

Dia. 112

Dia. 113

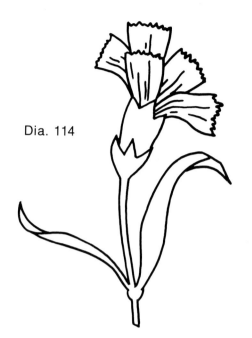

Dia. 114

Dia. 115

Dia. 116

Dia. 117

Dia. 118

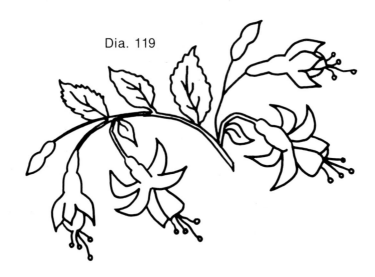

Dia. 119